Our Catholic Faith

A Summary of Basic Beliefs

◆ ◆ ◆ ◆ ◆

Rev. Msgr. John F. Barry

Official Theological Consultant
Most Rev. Edward K. Braxton, Ph.D., S.T.D.

William H. Sadlier, Inc.
9 Pine Street
New York, New York 10005-1002

Nihil Obstat
Reverend Eugenio Cárdenas, M.Sp.S.
Censor Deputatus

Imprimatur
✠ Cardinal Roger Mahony
Archbishop of Los Angeles
August 20, 1995

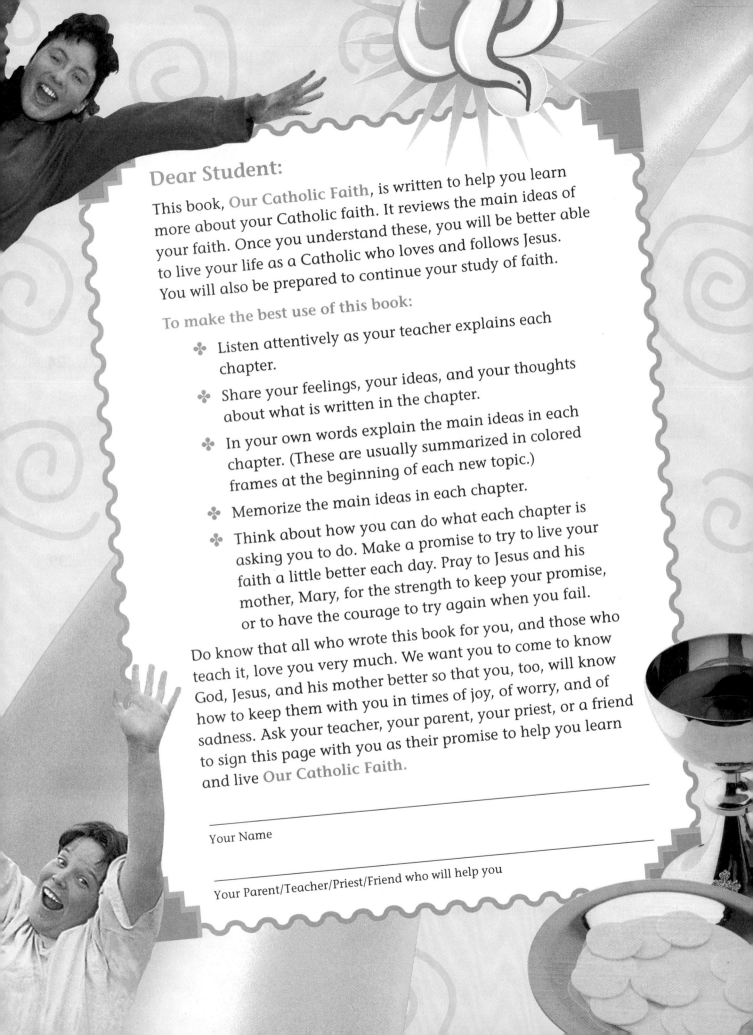

Dear Student:

This book, **Our Catholic Faith**, is written to help you learn more about your Catholic faith. It reviews the main ideas of your faith. Once you understand these, you will be better able to live your life as a Catholic who loves and follows Jesus. You will also be prepared to continue your study of faith.

To make the best use of this book:

- ❧ Listen attentively as your teacher explains each chapter.

- ❧ Share your feelings, your ideas, and your thoughts about what is written in the chapter.

- ❧ In your own words explain the main ideas in each chapter. (These are usually summarized in colored frames at the beginning of each new topic.)

- ❧ Memorize the main ideas in each chapter.

- ❧ Think about how you can do what each chapter is asking you to do. Make a promise to try to live your faith a little better each day. Pray to Jesus and his mother, Mary, for the strength to keep your promise, or to have the courage to try again when you fail.

Do know that all who wrote this book for you, and those who teach it, love you very much. We want you to come to know God, Jesus, and his mother better so that you, too, will know how to keep them with you in times of joy, of worry, and of sadness. Ask your teacher, your parent, your priest, or a friend to sign this page with you as their promise to help you learn and live **Our Catholic Faith.**

_____

Your Name

_____

Your Parent/Teacher/Priest/Friend who will help you

TABLE OF CONTENTS

UNIT IV

WE LIVE AS CATHOLICS

APPENDIX

1

God Is Our Creator

God Is Our Creator

When we look at a brilliant rainbow
  splashed across the summer sky…

Or hear the pounding of the waves
  against the shoreline…

Or smell the flowers,
  or hear a robin sing…

Or touch the new softness
  of a baby's hand…

When we stand in awe before
  the stars that light our universe…

**We praise and thank our God who
  made them all!**

VOCABULARY

divine
  a word used to describe God alone

original sin
  the sin of our first parents in
  which all of us share

What have you seen today that reminds you of God?

Describe what you saw in words or through art.

WE WILL LEARN

1 **God created the whole universe.**

2 **People turned away from God.**

3 **God promised to send a Savior.**

1 God created the whole universe.

The Bible is the greatest book ever written. It is the word of God and tells us about God and God's people. From the Bible we learn that everything in the universe was created by God.

After God created the world, God made human beings. In the Bible we read, "God created them in His own divine image. God created them male and female."
From Genesis 1:26–27

According to the Bible story, the first man and woman whom God made were Adam and Eve. God gave Adam and Eve charge over all creation and told them to care for it — the animals, flowers, trees, fish, even the running rivers and the deep oceans. All of creation was theirs to enjoy and protect. God wanted people to love and to be happy in the beautiful world He had made.

The whole story of creation is found in Genesis 1:1—2:4.

Name some of the things God created.

Who is supposed to care for God's world? Why?

Do You Know?

The Bible is really like a little library. It contains seventy-three small books. There are forty-six books in the Old Testament and twenty-seven books in the New Testament. The Old Testament was written before the time of Jesus. The first book of the Old Testament is the Book of Genesis.

The Bible helps us to learn who God is and how we have become His own people.

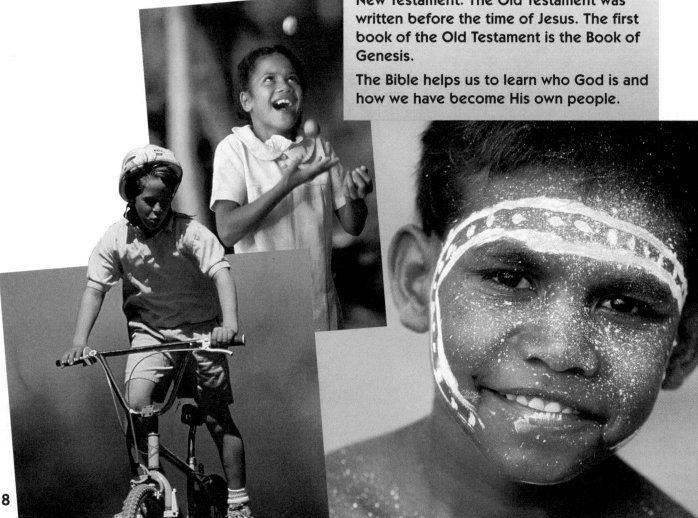

People turned away from God.

God created a world in which people would live in peace and joy. In God's plan, human beings would never be sick or die. They were created to be happy with God forever. That was God's plan for human beings.

God gave the first human beings wonderful gifts.

- ❧ They could feel and love.
- ❧ They could think and wonder.
- ❧ They could make things and explore.
- ❧ They could ask questions and seek answers.
- ❧ They could choose and decide.

One of God's greatest gifts to Adam and Eve was the gift of freedom. From the very beginning, they were free to choose either to do good or to do evil. God would not force them to do anything. God trusted them to act out of love rather than selfishness.

According to the Bible story, Adam and Eve did not live up to God's trust. They did not use their freedom wisely. They chose to act selfishly and to turn away from the loving God who had created them. When they chose to turn away from God, they sinned. This first sin is called *original sin*.

What do you think it means to use freedom wisely?

3 God promised to send a Savior.

Even though Adam and Eve sinned by disobeying God, God still loved them. He had a marvelous plan. God would send them someone who would save them from sin.

We know that this promised Savior was Jesus, the Son of God. Jesus would save all of us from sin and death. He would show us how to love God and one another.

God has given us the great gift of Jesus our Savior. Through Jesus, we can know how God wants us to live. We are to live now as friends of Jesus and to be happy with God forever in heaven.

What was God's plan to save us?

How can you show your love for God?

I Have Learned

Fill in the correct words.

God created people to be _____ with God forever.

Adam and Eve turned away from God. They chose to _____ .

God promised to send a _____ .

Prayer

Prayer is talking and listening to God. We can pray to thank God, to praise Him and to ask for His forgiveness. We can also ask God for all that we need. Here is a prayer praising God.

I will praise You, Lord, with all my heart; I will tell of all the wonderful things You have done!

From Psalm 9:1

I Will Do

Name some of the gifts God has given us.

Which one of these do you think is God's greatest gift to you?

How do you use this gift? What will you do to praise and thank God for this gift?

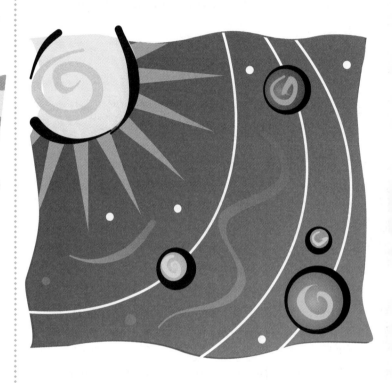

Remember

God created human beings and loved them even when they sinned.

God promised to send a Savior, to save all people from sin and death.

Review

1. What did God want people to do with the world He had created?
2. What did Adam and Eve choose to do?
3. Who is the Savior?

4. How does it make you feel to know that a loving God created and saved the world?

Family Note

In this lesson, your child has learned that our loving God created all things and that, in spite of people's sins, God sent Jesus to save us. Help your child to review the lesson by discussing the Remember and Review on this page.

Jesus Comes to Us

Being Alive!

What does it mean to be alive? It means we
have life and we can do special things.

We love.
We grow.
We share.
We laugh.
We have friends.
We think.
We understand.
We question.
We play.
We cry.
We learn.

Each of these things tells us something
about being human.

Which of these things are most important
to you now? Why?

VOCABULARY

incarnation
> the mystery of God "becoming
> flesh," or becoming one of us in
> Jesus

gospel
> the good news of God's love for us

kingdom of God
> the reign, or rule, of God in our
> hearts

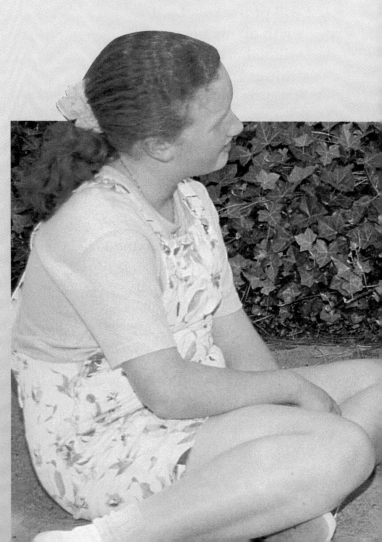

WE WILL LEARN

1 The Son of God was born into our human family.

2 In the gospels we read that Jesus was good to everyone.

3 Jesus preached about the kingdom of God.

1 The Son of God was born into our human family.

God's only Son became one of us. Jesus shared the same human experiences that we all have. He was like us in all things except that He never sinned.

The events surrounding Jesus' birth are described in the Bible. In the Gospel of Luke we read that one day the angel Gabriel brought a message to a Jewish girl named Mary. Gabriel told her that God wanted her to be the mother of Jesus. She did not understand how this could happen, but she believed and trusted in God.

Mary said yes to God's message. "I am the Lord's servant," said Mary. "May it happen to me as you have said."
From Luke 1:26–38

This event in Mary's life is called the *annunciation.* God's promise to send us a Savior was about to be fulfilled.

We celebrate the birth of Jesus on December 25, the feast of Christmas. Jesus is God's own Son. This mystery of God "becoming flesh," or becoming one of us in Jesus, is called the *incarnation.*

What do we mean by the incarnation?

What does it mean to you that the Son of God became a member of the human family?

DO YOU KNOW?

Each Sunday at Mass we hear a gospel reading from the Bible. The priest or deacon reads to us from the gospel according to Matthew, Mark, Luke, or John. We stand to hear the good news of Jesus Christ.

2 In the gospels we read that Jesus was good to everyone.

Jesus taught people to know and love God through His words and actions. The good things that Jesus did while He was on earth are described in the part of the Bible we call the four gospels. The word *gospel* means "good news." In one of the gospels we read, "He healed many people from their sicknesses, diseases, and evil spirits, and gave sight to many blind people."
From Luke 7:21

The good news of Jesus is that God loves, forgives, and cares for all of us. No one is left out.

In the gospels we read that Jesus taught us to love others as God loves us. Jesus did this by:

✤ feeding the hungry,

✤ curing the sick,

✤ forgiving sinners,

✤ being a friend to the poor,

✤ urging people to love God and one another.

Jesus called people to follow Him and share His work and teaching. "Come and follow Me," He said (from Mark 10:21).

Jesus asked twelve of His friends to be leaders of those who followed Him. We call these twelve the *apostles.* He placed Peter at their head. Jesus promised Peter, "You are a rock, and on this rock foundation I will build My Church" (from Matthew 16:18). The *Church* is the community Jesus founded.

What do we read in the gospels about the ways Jesus was good to everyone?

Name one way you can follow Jesus today.

3 Jesus preached about the kingdom of God.

Jesus was the one whom God had promised to send. He came to announce the coming of the kingdom of God, to establish His Church, and to free us from sin.

The kingdom of God is not a place. It is the reign, or rule, of God in our hearts. Jesus spoke often about this kingdom. He said it had begun in Him. All people are invited to become a part of the kingdom and to help build it. When we work and live for God's kingdom we look forward to being with God forever in heaven.

Jesus, the Son of God, is our model in living for God's kingdom. He taught us about God's kingdom in special stories called parables. In one parable, Jesus said that the kingdom was like a great treasure that people would want above all things. When we try to live as faithful followers of Jesus and as members of the Church, we turn away from sin and do what God asks. This is the way we live for God's kingdom.

What is the kingdom of God?

What must we do to share in God's kingdom?

God's Kingdom

I Have Learned

Write the number of the word in Column A next to the correct description in Column B.

Column A

1. annunciation
2. gospel
3. incarnation
4. kingdom of God

Column B

___ God's Son becoming one of us

___ the reign, or rule, of God in our hearts

___ good news of God's love

___ the announcement of the angel to Mary

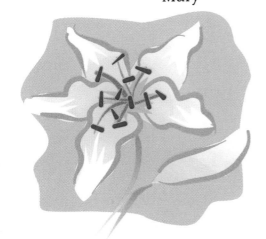

I Will Do

Here are some things I could do to work for God's kingdom:

- Love others.
- Be just and fair.
- Live in peace.
- Be a faithful member of Jesus' community, the Church.

Choose one of the above that you could do.

Explain how you could do it. Will you?

Prayer

It is good to ask God for the things that we need and for the help that only God can give us. Here is a prayer asking for God's help.

Jesus, Son of God,
help us to do good for everyone
as You did. Show us how to
work for God's kingdom in all
we do and say. Amen.

Remember

The Son of God became one of us to invite us to become part of God's kingdom.

In the gospels we read that Jesus was good to everyone.

Jesus is our Savior and shares with us the good news that God loves, forgives, and cares for all of us.

Review

1. What is the incarnation?
2. What is the good news of Jesus?
3. Name ways you can share in the kingdom of God.

4. How does it feel to know we have a Savior who knows how it feels to be human?

Family Note

The focus of this lesson is that Jesus Christ, the Son of God, was born into our human family and that He preached about the kingdom of God. Discuss with your child ways that we can all, in our everyday lives, work for God's kingdom. Close by praying together the prayer of this lesson.

Jesus Is Our Savior

New Life

"It's a girl! She's fine, and she's beautiful," shouted Dr. Jason through his surgical mask. He held up the newborn child for her happy parents to see.

As the doctor went to check on his other patients, he thought of that moment when he showed the baby to her parents.

Even though he had brought hundreds of babies into this world, that moment still thrilled him—seeing a new life at the instant of birth. It seemed like a miracle to him.

VOCABULARY

Holy Thursday
   the day on which we remember that Jesus gave us the Eucharist at the Last Supper

Good Friday
   the day on which we remember that Jesus died for us

Easter Sunday
   the day on which we celebrate the resurrection of Jesus from the dead

Dr. Jason's last stop was to visit a friend. Mr. Gregg was an elderly gentleman who was dying. Dr. Jason believed his friend would not live through the night. He stayed with the old man for a long time, making him as comfortable as possible. Suddenly Mr. Gregg opened his eyes. He smiled at Dr. Jason. Then the elderly man died.

That night Dr. Jason could not sleep. He thought about everything that had happened. In one day he had helped a baby be born. He had also helped a friend prepare for death and for the new life that was to come. Dr. Jason felt blessed.

Have you ever held a new baby?
How did it make you feel?

What do the words "new life" mean to you?

What does it mean to live forever?

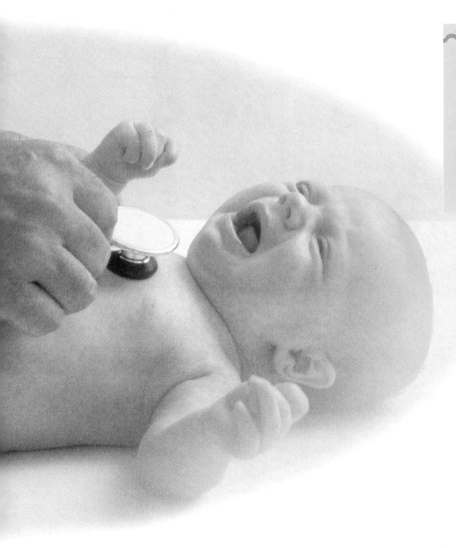

WE WILL LEARN

1 Jesus gave us the Eucharist at the Last Supper.

2 Jesus died on the cross for our salvation.

3 Jesus rose from the dead and brought us new life.

1 Jesus gave us the Eucharist at the Last Supper.

On the night before He died for us, Jesus gave us the gift of Himself. He did this at a special meal He had with His friends. We call this meal the Last Supper.

During the Last Supper, Jesus took bread and said, "Take this and eat it, for this is my body." Then Jesus took a cup of wine and said, "Drink this, for this is the cup of my blood, which will be shed for you. Do this in memory of me." We call this gift of Jesus' Body and Blood the *Eucharist*. Through this gift of Himself, Jesus would be truly present with His followers for all time.

Each year on Holy Thursday evening, we celebrate in a special way what Jesus did for us at the Last Supper. Whenever we participate in the Mass, we receive the Body and Blood of Christ in the Eucharist and are strengthened to live as Jesus' followers.

What did Jesus do on Holy Thursday?

Imagine you are at the Last Supper. How do you feel?

Do You Know?

Each year on Good Friday we remember that Jesus loved us so much that He was willing to suffer and die for us. In our homes and churches, we have crosses with the figure of Jesus on them. We call these crucifixes. They remind us that Jesus died for us. He is our Savior.

2 Jesus died on the cross for our salvation.

Jesus loved us so much that He was willing to die for us to save us from sin. After the Last Supper, Jesus went to pray in a garden with His friends. While they were there, Jesus was arrested by the authorities. They did not believe He was the Son of God. After beating Him and making fun of Him, some soldiers put a crown of thorns on Jesus' head. They forced Jesus to carry a heavy cross to Calvary, a hill outside Jerusalem. Jesus our Savior was crucified—nailed to a cross—and left to die. Even His followers abandoned Him.

While Jesus was nailed to the cross, He forgave those who had crucified Him. He prayed: "Father, forgive them; they do not know what they are doing."

From Luke 23:34

Jesus had often told His friends to forgive their enemies. Now, by His own example, He showed them the way to do this.

Why was Jesus crucified?

Have you ever forgiven someone who treated you unfairly? Tell about it.

3 Jesus rose from the dead and brought us new life.

Early on the Sunday morning after Jesus died, some women followers of Jesus went to the tomb in which He had been buried. It was empty! They thought someone had stolen Jesus' body. But Jesus had risen from the dead. Soon the risen Jesus appeared to His followers. They were filled with excitement and joy. Jesus was alive!

Through His death and resurrection, Jesus saved us from the power of sin and death. Jesus promised that His faithful followers would also share in His resurrection and have eternal life. Through Jesus, our risen Savior, we share in God's own life now and will live forever with God after our life on earth. We celebrate the feast of the resurrection on Easter Sunday.

For Catholics, the most important time of the year is the celebration of Jesus' saving death and resurrection. We call this time the *Easter Triduum*. Triduum means three days. The Easter Triduum begins with the Evening Mass of the Lord's Supper on Holy Thursday, continues through Good Friday and Holy Saturday, and ends with Evening Prayer on Easter Sunday.

What happened on Easter Sunday?

Explain the Easter Triduum.

I HAVE LEARNED

Complete the following.

On _____ _____
we remember that Jesus gave us the
Eucharist.

On _____ _____,
we remember that Jesus died on the

_____.

On _____ _____,
we celebrate that Jesus rose from the dead.

We call Jesus' rising to new life after death

the _____.

What does "new life" mean to you now?

Why do you think Easter is so important?

I WILL DO

Each Sunday is like Easter. When we
celebrate the Eucharist, we remember that
Jesus died for us and rose from the dead.

How will you try to remember this the next
time you go to church?

PRAYER

The Church often gives us words to use
when we pray. When we pray together as
members of God's family, we use the prayers
of the Church. Here is a prayer we pray on
Good Friday.

**We adore You, O Christ, and we bless
You, because by Your Holy Cross You
have redeemed the world.**

Remember

Jesus gave us the Eucharist at the Last
Supper.

Jesus died on the cross and rose from the
dead. He is our Savior.

Review

1. What did Jesus do at the Last Supper?
2. Why did Jesus die?
3. What do we call the day Jesus rose from
   the dead?

Unit 1 Test

Complete each sentence.

1. The good news of God's love for us is the

   _____.

2. A name for God, who made our universe and everything in it, is

   _____.

3. The sin of our first parents, in which we all share, is

   _____.

4. The day on which we remember that Jesus gave us the Eucharist is

   _____.

5. The reign, or rule, of God in our hearts is called the

   _____.

6. A cross with the figure of Jesus on it is called a

   _____.

7. The day on which we remember that Jesus rose from the dead is

   _____.

8. The book of the word of God is the

   _____.

9. The mystery of God becoming one of us in Jesus is the

   _____.

10. The day on which we remember that Jesus died for us is

    _____.

Put the biblical events in the order in which they happened, using numbers 1 through 10.

11. God promised to send a Savior. ____

12. Jesus rose from the dead on Easter Sunday. ____

13. Jesus, God's own Son, became one of us. ____

14. Jesus forgave those who crucified Him. ____

15. Jesus made Saint Peter head of the apostles. ____

16. Mary said yes to God's message. ____

17. Jesus asked twelve of His friends to be apostles, leaders of those who followed Him. ____

18. Jesus died on Good Friday. ____

19. The angel Gabriel brought a message from God to Mary. ____

20. At the Last Supper on Holy Thursday, Jesus gave us the Eucharist. ____

Write the word or phrase that best completes each sentence.

21. God created _____ in God's image.

22. God created a _____ where people would live in

_____ and joy.

23. Jesus promised that we will share in His resurrection and have

_____ when we die.

24. Jesus became one of us to show us how to live for _____.

25. Think first, then answer these questions. What is the good news of Jesus? What does it mean to you?

_____

_____

_____

_____

_____

_____

4

Jesus Sends the Holy Spirit

A Call for Help

Some years ago a young man, poor and discouraged, stopped by his parish church to pray. The young man wanted to be a comedian, to make people laugh, to bring joy to the lives of others. But the young man could not get a job—he was an unknown, and no one would hire him. That night he prayed to Saint Jude. He asked for help to get started in the career that he knew was right for him. His name was Danny Thomas.

VOCABULARY

Blessed Trinity
the three Persons in one God: God the Father, God the Son, and God the Holy Spirit

Church
the community of the baptized followers of Jesus Christ

Holy Spirit
God, the third Person of the Blessed Trinity

Danny Thomas went on to become a well-loved and successful performer in movies and on television. In gratitude to Saint Jude, he built a cancer hospital for children and named it in honor of the saint. Danny Thomas has died, but his work for children continues.

Have you ever received help when you really needed it? Tell about it.

WE WILL LEARN

1 Jesus promised to send the Holy Spirit to His followers.

2 The Holy Spirit came on Pentecost.

3 The Holy Spirit helps the Church to grow.

ST. JUDE HOSPITAL

DANNY THOMAS
FOUNDER
1960

1 Jesus promised to send the Holy Spirit to His followers.

Jesus knew that people would need help in living as He had asked them to live. The night before He died, Jesus promised His followers that He would send them a Helper, the Holy Spirit. The Holy Spirit, the third Person of the Blessed Trinity, would stay with them forever. The Holy Spirit would teach them and help them to remember all that Jesus had told them (from John 14:16, 26).

After Jesus rose from the dead, He stayed with His friends for a while, teaching and helping them. He told them to bring the good news of God's love to all the world. Jesus said, "Remember, I will be with you always, until the end of time."
Matthew 28:19–20

Forty days after Easter, Jesus returned to His Father in heaven. Jesus' return to heaven is called the *ascension*. His followers, meanwhile, waited for the coming of the Holy Spirit, whom Jesus had promised.

Why did Jesus promise to send the Holy Spirit to His followers?

How do you think Jesus' followers felt about His promise?

2 The Holy Spirit came on Pentecost.

On the Jewish feast of Pentecost, the followers of Jesus were together, praying and waiting for the Holy Spirit. As they prayed, something astounding happened.

In the Bible we read: "Suddenly there was a noise from the sky. It sounded like a strong wind blowing, and it filled the whole house where they were sitting. Then they saw what looked like tongues of fire that spread out and touched each person there. They were all filled with the Holy Spirit. They began to speak in many languages about Jesus and the great things God had done through Him."
From Acts 2:1–4

That day several thousand people were baptized into the community of Jesus and received the gift of the Holy Spirit. They became members of the Church.

The day the Holy Spirit came to the followers of Jesus is called *Pentecost.* Today we celebrate Pentecost as the birthday of the Church.

Why do you think Pentecost is called the "birthday of the Church"?

Do You Know?

When we follow the guidance of the Holy Spirit, we develop certain qualities known as the twelve fruits of the Holy Spirit. These qualities are charity, joy, peace, patience, kindness, goodness, generosity, gentleness, faithfulness, modesty, self-control, and chastity.

The Holy Spirit helps the Church to grow.

Pentecost was the beginning of a new life for the little group of Jesus' followers. The Holy Spirit filled them with courage and love and helped them to share the good news of Jesus Christ with everyone.

More and more people asked to be baptized. They wanted to follow Jesus and to be part of His community, the Church. They gathered together to pray and to celebrate the Eucharist in His memory and to celebrate the presence of the risen Christ among them. People began to call the followers of Jesus Christ "Christians."

The early Christians tried to live according to the teachings of Jesus. The rich shared what they had with the poor. Those who were well took care of the sick or handicapped.

People said of them, "See how these Christians love one another!"

As Catholics, we know that the Church continues to grow. Each of us receives the Holy Spirit for the first time when we become members of the Church at Baptism. The Holy Spirit helps us to live as followers of Jesus and still guides the Church today.

How did the Holy Spirit help the early Church?

How would you like the Holy Spirit to help you?

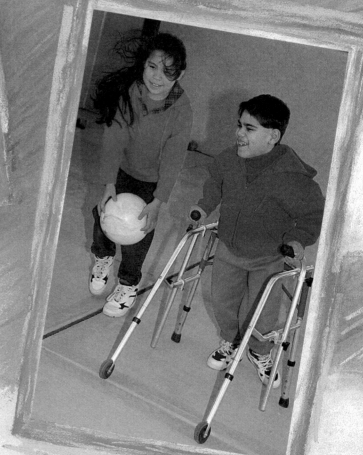

I Have Learned

Reread the Bible story of the first Pentecost in Acts of the Apostles 2:1–11. Tell what happened as if you were there.

Imagine yourself telling a friend about God's love for people as shown on the first Pentecost. What would you say?

I Will Do

Think about the story you have told. What one thing will you do this week to show you are happy to be a member of the Church?

PRAYER

The Church invites us to begin our prayer with the Sign of the Cross. We make the sign of the cross by placing our right hand on our forehead, chest, and on each shoulder while saying the following: In the name of the Father, and of the Son, and of the Holy Spirit. Amen.

Here is a prayer to the Holy Spirit:

Come, Holy Spirit, fill our hearts with the fire of Your love. Amen.

Remember

Jesus promised to send the Holy Spirit to His followers.

The Holy Spirit came to the followers of Jesus on Pentecost.

The Holy Spirit still guides the Church today.

Review

1. Why did Jesus promise to send the Holy Spirit to His followers?
2. When did the Holy Spirit come to the followers of Jesus?
3. How did the Holy Spirit change the followers of Jesus?
4. How might the Holy Spirit help you to change?

Family Note

This lesson focuses on Jesus' promise of the Spirit, on Pentecost, and on the growth of the early Church. Review with your child the story of the first Pentecost, and then let your child share his or her story from the **I Have Learned** activity.

5

The Catholic Church Today

Every Sunday Morning

Jerry sat at the window, looking at the Catholic church across the street. Jerry was not a Catholic, but he liked to get up early on Sunday mornings and watch the neighborhood slowly come to life.

He had seen the same scenes unfold every Sunday morning since his family had moved here. Every few hours the parish church bells would ring, and then people would start to come. They would come by car, bus, or on foot; alone, in pairs, or with their families. A new group came every few hours until well after noon.

What, Jerry wondered, brought them to this church? What did they find there that made them come?

VOCABULARY

pope
the bishop of Rome, the successor of Saint Peter who leads and serves the whole Church

bishops
the successors of the apostles

worship
to praise and honor God

How would you answer Jerry's questions?

If you took Jerry to your church, what would you point out to him first?

WE WILL LEARN

1 The Church worships and serves throughout the world.

2 The Church is one, holy, catholic, and apostolic.

3 The apostolic leaders of the Church are the pope and bishops.

1 The Church worships and serves throughout the world.

The members of the Catholic Church gather to worship in churches all over the world.

In our parish churches, we are surrounded by reminders of God and the things of God. The altar is a symbol of Christ and the place where Mass is celebrated. Statues of Jesus, Mary, Joseph, and the saints, as well as candles, and stations of the cross are reminders of our fellowship with holy people and holy things. Most important of all, Jesus Himself is really present in the Blessed Sacrament, which is kept in the tabernacle.

No one is excluded from belonging to the Catholic Church. Men, women, old people and children, members of all nationalities and races, and people who speak different languages are all welcome. All of us gather to pray to God together. We listen to God's word from the Bible and offer thanks and praise to Him at Mass.

Our worship of God strengthens us to love and serve others. Together we go forth to bring the message of God's kingdom to the world.

Who can belong to the Catholic Church?

How can the Church help new members feel at home?

2 The Church is one, holy, catholic, and apostolic.

The Holy Spirit helped the early Church to follow Christ and to love and serve others. The Holy Spirit continues to help the Church today.

We are members of the Catholic Church. There are four great identifying marks that show the kind of community Jesus founded. We say that the Church is *one, holy, catholic,* and *apostolic.*

We believe that the Church is *one.* We profess the same creed. We receive the same sacraments. We are united by the leadership of the pope and bishops.

The Church is *holy.* This means that the Church shares with all people the holiness of Jesus Christ. The Church helps us to grow in holiness, especially through prayer, good works, and the sacraments.

The Church is *catholic,* which means that it is open to all and has a message for all people. Catholics believe that all people are invited to be followers of Jesus. No one should be left out. The Church is for all people everywhere.

As Catholics, we believe that the Church is *apostolic.* This means that the Church was founded on the apostles. Today the pope carries on the work of Saint Peter. The other bishops carry on the work of the first apostles.

DO YOU KNOW?

All the baptized followers of Jesus Christ carry on His work in the world. We are all members of the Church. However, those who are ordained are called to a special ministry of service in the Church.

In your own words, tell what the words *one, holy, catholic,* and *apostolic* mean to you?

What can you do to show you are proud to belong to the Catholic Church?

35

3 The apostolic leaders of the Church are the pope and bishops.

Jesus named Peter to be the first leader of the Church. He wanted Peter and the other apostles to teach others all that He had taught them.

Today our pope and bishops, who follow in the steps of Peter and the apostles, are called the *successors* to the apostles. This means that, with the help of the Holy Spirit, they teach, serve, lead, and make holy the Church, just as Peter and the apostles did. They lead us in the way of holiness and truth.

Our Holy Father the pope is the successor of Saint Peter and the leader of the whole Catholic Church.

What is the name of our present pope?

Bishops are the successors of the apostles. Today most bishops teach, serve, and lead large parts of the Catholic Church called *dioceses*.

Name your diocese.
Name your bishop.

Priests and deacons are ordained ministers of the Church who teach, serve, and lead in our *parishes*.

Name your parish.
Name your pastor and the other priests and deacons in your parish.

Each of us is united with our pope, bishops, priests, and deacons in living out our faith.

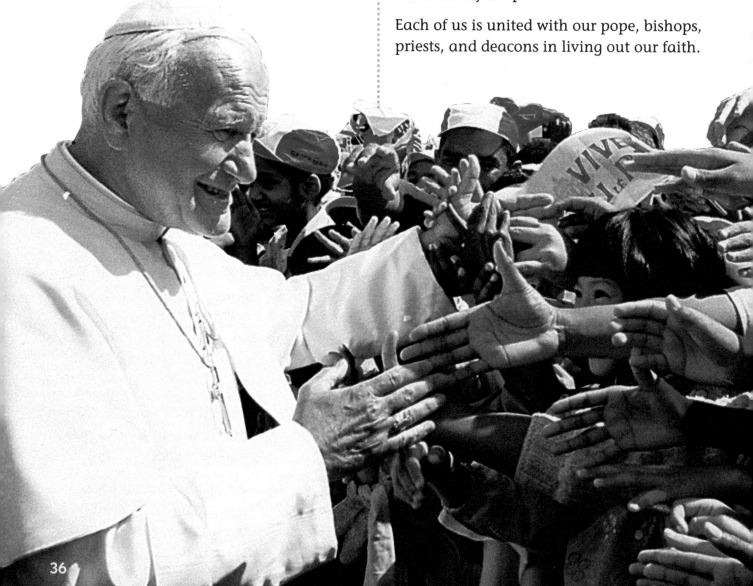

I HAVE LEARNED

Write the number of the word next to the correct description.

1. catholic   ___ is the successor of Saint Peter

2. pope   ___ the Church is for all people

3. bishops   ___ the Church shares the holiness of Jesus

4. holy   ___ are the successors of the apostles

PRAYER

Sometimes we pray prayers from the Bible. Here is one of them.

I love the house where you live, O Lord, the place where your glory dwells.

Psalm 26:8

I WILL DO

I will remember that as a Catholic I have been called to help and serve other people as Jesus did.

This week, I will help

_____
(name)

by:

_____ .

Remember

The Church worships and serves throughout the world.

The Church is one, holy, catholic, and apostolic.

The apostolic leaders of the Church are the pope and bishops.

Review

1. Describe what it means to belong to the Catholic Church.

2. Name the four marks of the Church.

3. How are the pope and bishops like Saint Peter and the apostles?

Family Note

This lesson describes what it means to say that the Church is one, holy, catholic, and apostolic. Encourage your child to carry out his or her decision to love and serve someone special this week.

6

The Seven Sacraments

Vocabulary

sign
something we see, hear, touch, or taste that stands for something else and points to something more important

sacrament
a powerful sign through which Jesus shares God's life and love with us in the community of the Church

Celebrating Together

We all enjoy celebrations. We often get together with our family and friends to celebrate important times in our lives.

Look at the chart on this page. Talk about the things that we can see and hear at different celebrations. Tell why each celebration is taking place.

You will notice an empty box in the Thanksgiving celebration. Write in it something you might see on this day.

Celebration	Signs We See
Birthday	candles, cake
Thanksgiving	_____
_____	_____

Choose one other time that your family celebrates—for example, Christmas. Write the name of the celebration on the chart. Talk about what you see and hear, and then tell why you celebrate.

Imagine what life would be like without celebrations. How would you feel?

Signs We Hear

"Happy Birthday to you"

"Happy Thanksgiving"

_____

Why We Celebrate

We tell someone we are happy that he or she was born.

We thank God for all God's gifts.

_____

1 Jesus used signs to show His love.

Jesus often used signs to show people how deeply He loved them. Jesus touched sick people and healed them. He was kind to lonely people and made them happy. He forgave those who were sorry for their sins. He gave people life.

By everything Jesus said and did, He showed us the power of God's love.

In what special ways did Jesus show people that He loved them?

The Catholic Church celebrates seven sacraments.

The Catholic Church has seven powerful signs through which Jesus Christ shares God's life and love with us. We call these signs sacraments. These signs are unlike any other signs in our lives. This is because when we celebrate them, Jesus shares with us God's own life of grace.

 **The Seven Sacraments**

Sacraments We Celebrate	Signs We See	Signs We Hear	Why We Celebrate
Baptism	water	"I baptize you in the name of the Father...."	Jesus shares God's life with us and we become members of the Church.
Confirmation	anointing with oil	"Be sealed with the Gift of the Holy Spirit."	Jesus sends the Holy Spirit to strengthen us in a special way.
Eucharist	bread and wine	"This is my body. This is my blood."	Jesus shares His Body and Blood with us.
Reconciliation	priest makes the sign of the cross	"I absolve you from your sins...."	Jesus forgives those who are sorry.
Anointing of the Sick	priest anoints sick person	"Through this holy anointing may the Lord in his love and mercy help you...."	Jesus comforts and strengthens those who are sick.
Matrimony	joining of hands	"I take you for my lawful wife (or husband)...."	Jesus blesses the love of a man and a woman.
Holy Orders	bishop lays his hands on head of person being ordained	silence, followed by a special prayer for the person ordained	Jesus calls bishops, priests, and deacons to be the ordained ministers of the Church.

Choose three of the above sacraments. In your own words, describe each one.
Use the chart to help you.

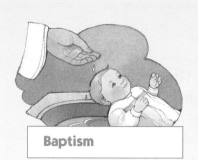

Baptism

Confirmation

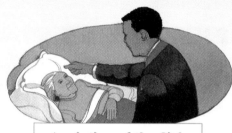

Eucharist

Matrimony

Reconciliation

Holy Orders

Anointing of the Sick

3 The sacraments are life-giving signs.

The sacraments are more than ordinary signs—they are life-giving signs. This is because they give us a share in God's life. God's life and love in us is called *grace*. Grace is a sharing in the divine life, in God's very life and love.

By celebrating the seven sacraments, the Church worships and praises God. Through these powerful signs, the Church itself becomes a sign of Jesus' presence in the world.

We are invited to carry out the mission of Jesus in the world. We respond to the sacraments by the way we live our lives.

Talk about one of the sacraments that you have received.

How has receiving this sacrament made a difference in your life?

DO YOU KNOW?

Here are the names of the seven sacraments that we celebrate in the Catholic Church.

These three sacraments are known as the sacraments of initiation:
- ❖ Baptism
- ❖ Confirmation
- ❖ Eucharist

These two sacraments are known as the sacraments of healing:
- ❖ Reconciliation
- ❖ Anointing of the Sick

These two sacraments are known as the sacraments of service:
- ❖ Matrimony
- ❖ Holy Orders

I HAVE LEARNED

Do the puzzle.

_____ are life-giving _____
     1   2

given to us by Jesus _____.
                            3

God's life in us is called _____.
                                  4

Each sacrament has signs we can

_____, _____, touch or taste.
      5   6

I WILL DO

Talk to a friend or family member about the sacraments. Use the chart on text page 41 to help you.

When you meet Jesus in the sacraments, what would you like your response to be?

PRAYER

Before we pray, we should stop, be quiet, and think about what we are going to do. Do that now before you pray.

God our Father, You have given us the gifts of the sacraments so that Your Church may grow in holiness. In each sacrament we meet Jesus, who shares with us Your life of grace. Help us to know and appreciate these great gifts. We ask this through Jesus Christ, Your Son, our Lord. Amen.

Remember

The sacraments are powerful signs through which Jesus shares God's life and love with us in the community of the Church.

Review

1. What is a sacrament?
2. Name the seven sacraments.
3. Think about the next time you will celebrate Eucharist or Reconciliation.

What can you do to prepare yourself better for these sacraments?

~ Family Note ~

In this lesson your child has learned that sacraments are life-giving signs through which Jesus shares God's life of grace with us. Help your child with this lesson by providing any pictures you have of family members celebrating the sacraments.

Unit II Test

Complete each sentence.

1. The baptized followers of Jesus Christ are called

   _____.

2. The successor of Saint Peter and the leader of the whole Church is the

   _____.

3. Something we taste, hear, touch, or see that stands for something else is a

   _____.

4. God the third Person of the Blessed Trinity is the

   _____.

5. Jesus' return to heaven is called the

   _____.

6. The successors of the apostles are the

   _____.

7. The community of the baptized followers of Jesus Christ is the

   _____.

8. We become members of the Church through the sacrament of

   _____.

9. On Pentecost the Holy Spirit came to the

   _____.

10. Jesus shares God's life of grace with us through the

    _____.

Answer the questions.

11. What are the names of the sacraments of initiation?

    _____

    _____

    _____

12. What do we mean when we say the Church is catholic?

    _____

    _____

13. What are the names of the sacraments of healing?

    _____

    _____

14. What is it the Holy Spirit helps the Church to do?

    _____

15. What are the names of the sacraments of service?

    _____

    _____

Complete each sentence.

16. Jesus told His followers to bring the _____

_____ of God's love to all the world.

17. After Jesus' ascension, His followers waited for the coming of the

_____ _____.

18. Jesus had promised to send a _____ who would teach
and guide His followers forever.

19. The _____ are signs that the Church celebrates to

_____ and praise God.

20. There are _____ sacraments.

21. We celebrate _____ as the birthday of the Church.

22. The marks of the Church are _____, _____,

catholic and _____.

23. In each of the sacraments Jesus shares God's _____ with us.

24. Why are the pope and the bishops so important in the Church?

_____

_____

25. How do your actions show that you are a follower of Jesus?

_____

_____

_____

Summary One Test

Complete each sentence by circling the letter of the correct ending.

1. The word *gospel* means
   a. "Follow Me."
   b. good news.
   c. read the Bible daily.
   d. say your prayers every Sunday.

2. On the night before Jesus died, He promised to send a Helper. That Helper was
   a. Mary.
   b. the pope.
   c. the Holy Spirit.
   d. the angel Gabriel.

3. In God's plan, human beings would
   a. never have to think.
   b. be forced to do God's will.
   c. become sick and die.
   d. be happy with God forever.

4. To say that the Church is *apostolic* means that
   a. our pope and bishops continue the work of Jesus and the apostles.
   b. it is a small church.
   c. its members are leaders.
   d. it is 3000 years old.

5. Through the angel Gabriel, God asked Mary to
   a. pray in the morning.
   b. become the mother of God's Son.
   c. be silent.
   d. fear the angel.

6. At Pentecost the Holy Spirit filled the disciples with
   a. laughter.
   b. fear.
   c. rules.
   d. courage and love.

7. When Jesus told His friends how to treat their enemies, He told them to
   a. hate their enemies.
   b. forgive them.
   c. ignore them.
   d. fight them.

8. The sacraments of initiation are Baptism, Confirmation, and
   a. Anointing of the Sick.
   b. Holy Orders.
   c. Eucharist.
   d. Reconciliation.

9. The sacraments of healing are Reconciliation and
   a. Anointing of the Sick.
   b. Eucharist.
   c. Matrimony.
   d. Baptism.

10. Jesus' return to His Father in heaven is called
    a. Easter morning.
    b. Pentecost.
    c. Good Friday.
    d. the ascension.

Complete the following quotations with words from the list. After each quotation write who said it.

with	follow	doing	happen	me
Remember	am	Father	servant	forgive
Me	you	always	end	

11. "Let it _____ to _____ as _____ have said."

_____

12. " _____, _____ them, they do not know what they are

_____ ." _____

13. " _____ , I will be _____ you _____ until the

_____ of time." _____

14. "I _____ the Lord's _____ ."

_____

15. "Come, _____ _____ ."

_____

Complete each sentence by circling the letter of the correct ending.

16. The Blessed Trinity is
   a. not hard to understand.
   b. three divine Persons in one God.
   c. a sacrament.
   d. a promise.

17. The sacraments are
   a. powerful signs of God's life and love.
   b. rules that we follow.
   c. names for the Church.
   d. celebrations of holy days.

18. The Bible is
   a. just for priests and lectors.
   b. a book of scientific facts.
   c. the book of God's word.
   d. a gift of the Holy Spirit.

19. The kingdom of God is
   a. a beautiful place in the sky.
   b. the reign, or rule, of God in our hearts.
   c. a corporal work of mercy.
   d. Peter and the apostles.

20. Think first, then answer this question. Are you happy to be a member of the Catholic Church? Tell why. (Use another piece of paper if you need to.)

_____

_____

7

Becoming Catholic

A New Member of the Church!

Tom and Ellen Matthews were as happy as they had been on their wedding day two years earlier. Once again they were surrounded by their family and friends in Holy Child Church. This time, all eyes were on their new baby, Michael. Soon the priest would enter the church, welcome everyone, and the celebration would begin.

"Just think, Tom," whispered Ellen, "in a few minutes, Michael will be baptized."

VOCABULARY

Baptism
   the sacrament by which we are freed from sin, become children of God, and are welcomed as members of the Church

Confirmation
   the sacrament in which the Holy Spirit comes to us in a special way to give us courage to live as Jesus' disciples

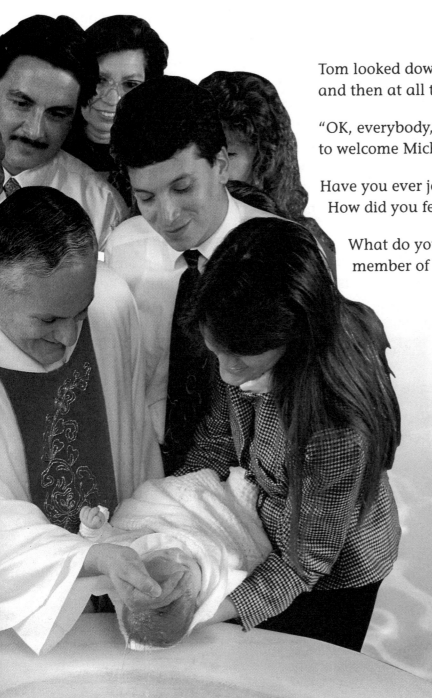

Tom looked down at the tiny face of the baby and then at all the smiling faces around them.

"OK, everybody," he said proudly. "Let's all get ready to welcome Michael as a new member of the Church."

Have you ever joined a new group? How did you feel when you were welcomed?

What do you think it means to be a baptized member of the Church?

WE WILL LEARN

1 We become members of the Church through Baptism.

2 Baptism frees us from sin.

3 Confirmation makes us strong in our faith.

We become members of the Church through Baptism.

Baptism is an exciting moment. It is a time of welcoming and joy as someone becomes a member of the Church. But Baptism is much more than simply a welcoming. It is the first of the sacraments of initiation—Baptism, Confirmation, and Eucharist—and the beginning of new life with God in the community of the Church.

At Baptism we become children of God. We are given a share in God's very life, which we call grace. By Baptism we are united with Jesus in His death and resurrection. We die to sin and rise to new life, as Jesus did.

Baptism is a rebirth into God's life. It changes us forever, and that is why we are only baptized once.

At the beginning of the rite of Baptism, the priest or deacon welcomes us in the name of the whole Christian community. During the ceremony, the priest or deacon pours water over the head of the person being baptized or immerses that person in the baptismal water. As he does this he says, "(_Name_), I baptize you in the name of the Father, and of the Son, and of the Holy Spirit." The water and these words are the signs of the sacrament of Baptism.

Because most of us were baptized as infants, our parents and godparents promised to help us to grow each day as faithful followers of

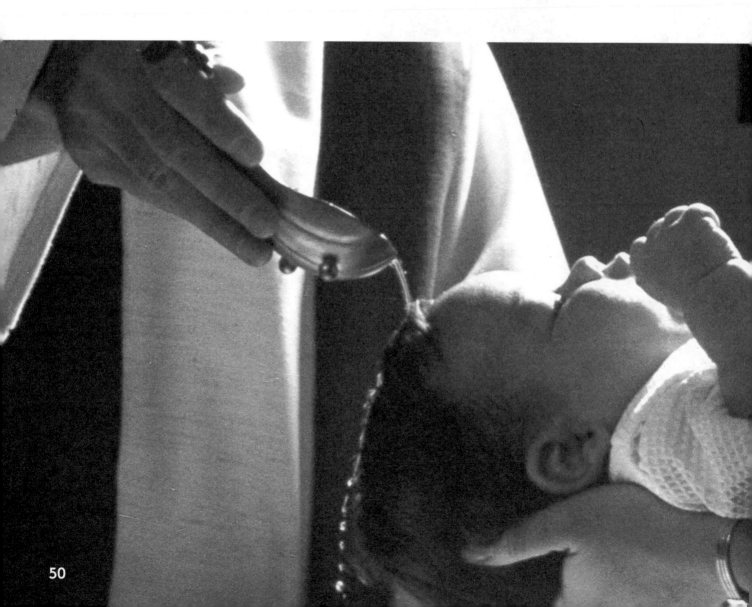

Jesus Christ and members of the Church. When we are old enough, we must make this choice and renew our baptismal promises for ourselves.

Why are we baptized only once?

What are the signs of the sacrament of Baptism?

2 Baptism frees us from sin.

At Baptism we are signed with the sign of the cross. This reminds us that we belong to Christ, who came to save us from sin. Through Baptism, we are freed from sin, both original sin and any personal sins we may have committed.

Original sin is the sin of our first parents. Every human being is born with and suffers from the effects of this sin. This means that all human beings have a tendency to sin, to choose what is against God's law. The grace of Baptism helps us to resist the effects of original sin. Baptism frees us from sin and enables us to do God's will.

What is original sin?

What does the grace of Baptism do for us?

DO YOU KNOW?

We are baptized in the name of the three Persons in God—God the Father, God the Son, and God the Holy Spirit. The Blessed Trinity is the basic truth of our Christian faith. It means that we believe that there are three Persons in one God.

3 Confirmation strengthens us in our faith.

The sacrament of Confirmation is the second sacrament of initiation. When we are confirmed, God the Holy Spirit comes to us as our Helper and Guide so that we might be true and faithful witnesses of Christ. In this sacrament, the person being confirmed is sealed, or anointed, with holy oil. Ordinarily a bishop confirms and when doing so says, "Be sealed with the Gift of the Holy Spirit." Just as in Baptism, Confirmation is given only once. From the moment of Confirmation, we are sealed with the Holy Spirit for a lifetime.

When we are confirmed, the Holy Spirit strengthens us with special gifts that help us live as faithful followers and witnesses of Jesus Christ. These gifts are: wisdom, understanding, right judgment, courage, knowledge, reverence, and wonder and awe. You can look up these words in the *Glossary* under the entry *Gifts of the Holy Spirit*.

Baptism and Confirmation are two of the three sacraments of initiation. Through these sacraments we begin and celebrate our membership in the Church. In the next lesson we will learn about the third sacrament of initiation, the Eucharist. This sacrament will nourish us for a lifetime.

What does the Holy Spirit do for us in Confirmation?

What can confirmed Catholics do to show they are followers of Jesus?

courage
knowledge
reverence
wonder & awe
wisdom
understanding
right judgment

I HAVE LEARNED

Circle the correct answer.

The first sacrament of initiation is
- ❖ Baptism.
- ❖ Confirmation.
- ❖ Holy Orders.

Baptism frees us from
- ❖ God's life.
- ❖ death.
- ❖ original sin.

Confirmation makes us
- ❖ faithful followers of Jesus.
- ❖ forget about others.
- ❖ share our faith only with our family.

In Baptism we are welcomed into
- ❖ a club.
- ❖ the Church.
- ❖ our school.

Why must you learn as much as you can about being a Catholic?

What do you like most about being a member of the Church?

I WILL DO

Find out all you can about your own Baptism. Does your family have any pictures to recall that special day?

Who are your godparents? Write their names here.

_____

_____

PRAYER

Each sacrament is a great prayer. When we celebrate the sacraments, we are praying with the whole Church. Let us thank God for the sacraments.

Father, we thank You for the sacraments, which are signs of Your unseen power.

Help us to keep alive the light of faith in us. Make us true witnesses to You and to Your love for us. We ask this through Jesus Christ our Lord. Amen.

Remember

In Baptism we are freed from sin, become children of God, and are welcomed as members of the Church.

In Confirmation the Holy Spirit comes to us in a special way.

Review

1. What happens in the sacrament of Baptism?

2. What does the Holy Spirit strengthen us to do in Confirmation?

3. What can you do to share your faith with others?

Family Note

In this lesson, your child has learned about the sacraments of Baptism and Confirmation. Encourage him or her to spend time talking with you about what it means to be baptized and confirmed.

8

The Sacrament of the Eucharist

The Best Gift

How exciting it is to find a gift with your name on it. Everyone loves to open a gift and find out what is inside.

When we love people we want to choose the best gifts for them. We look for things that will make them happy.

There are some gifts that cannot be put in a box. We cannot put a smile in a box, but a smile is a wonderful gift. We cannot tie a bow on a hug, but a hug is a wonderful gift.

VOCABULARY

Eucharist
the sacrament of the Body and Blood of Christ

Mass
our celebration of the Eucharist and our greatest prayer of thanks and praise to God

The best gift we can give others is ourselves! When we love others, we give them our love and our time. We listen to their stories. We cry with them when they are sad. We laugh with them when they are happy.

What is the best gift you have ever received? Why?

Have you ever thought of yourself as a gift? In what way?

WE WILL LEARN

1 **Jesus gave us Himself in the Eucharist.**

2 **We celebrate the Eucharist at Mass.**

3 **The Eucharist is both a sacrifice and a meal.**

1 Jesus gave us Himself in the Eucharist.

The sacrament of the Eucharist is at the very heart and center of Catholic life. It is also the third of the sacraments of initiation. The word *Eucharist* means "to give thanks." When we celebrate this sacrament, we give thanks to God for the greatest gift we can ever receive, the gift of Jesus Himself.

When Jesus was with His apostles, He called Himself the Bread of Life. Jesus was always caring for others, healing the sick, and forgiving sinners. He wanted us to love one another as He loved us. The greatest sign of His love was that He offered His life for our sins. He sacrificed Himself for us. He saved us by His suffering, death, and resurrection.

We know that Jesus wanted us to remember His love and to be with us always. That is why He gave us the Eucharist, the gift of Himself, at the Last Supper on the night before He died. When He gave us His Body and Blood, Jesus said to do this in memory of Him.

Ever since that Last Supper, the community of the Church has continued to celebrate the Eucharist in memory of Jesus. At Mass we offer bread and wine to God. Through the words and actions of the priest and the power of the Holy Spirit, the bread and wine become the Body and Blood of Christ.

Jesus continues to give Himself to us in this great sacrament. When we receive Holy Communion, we receive the Body and Blood of Christ.

What gift did Jesus give us at the Last Supper?

Why do we continue to celebrate the Eucharist?

The Last Supper, **Philipe de Champaigne, circa 1648**

2 We celebrate the Eucharist at Mass.

After the death and resurrection of Jesus, His friends often came together to pray and to remember what Jesus had told them. They came to know that the risen Jesus was with them in the Breaking of the Bread, another name they used for the Eucharist. They shared the Body and Blood of Christ under the appearances of bread and wine. They were happy that Jesus still remained with them in the Eucharist.

Today, the friends of Jesus still celebrate the Eucharist together. The priest says the words over the bread and wine that Jesus said at the Last Supper. The bread and wine become Jesus' Body and Blood. Jesus gives us the gift of Himself to nourish us and to help us live as members of His Church.

The celebration of the Eucharist is called the *Mass*. The Mass is our great prayer of praise and thanks to God. That is why the Church requires that all Catholics join with others to take part in the Mass every Saturday evening or Sunday.

When we take part in our parish celebration of the Eucharist, we show that we appreciate the great gift Jesus has given us—the gift of Himself.

What did Jesus ask His friends to do during the Last Supper?

Why should we take part in the Mass every Saturday evening or Sunday and as often as we can during the week?

Do You Know?

As a sign of respect and to remind us of the spiritual nourishment we are about to receive, the Church asks us not to take any food or drink (except water or medicine) for one hour before receiving Holy Communion. We call this the eucharistic fast.

3 The Eucharist is both a sacrifice and a meal.

The Eucharist is both a sacrifice and a meal. In the Eucharist we share in the sacrifice of Christ. We give thanks and celebrate Jesus' death and resurrection. In this sacrifice of praise to God, we remember all that Jesus did for us. In the Eucharist we offer ourselves with Jesus to God. When we celebrate the Eucharist, we pray to the Father, through the Son, in the unity of the Holy Spirit.

The sacrament of the Eucharist is also a sacred meal. In this sacrament we receive the gift of Jesus, who gave Himself to us as our food. Jesus is really present in the Eucharist. Sharing in the Eucharist makes us one with God and with all the members of the Church.

We assemble as Jesus' community of disciples to celebrate the Eucharist at Mass. We remember that Jesus loved us so much that He sacrificed Himself for us and died on the cross to save us from our sins. Through the Eucharist we become a living sacrifice of praise.

We remember that Jesus rose from the dead and now remains with us in the Eucharist. We give thanks to Jesus for the gift of Himself by living as His disciples.

How is the Eucharist a meal? a sacrifice?

Why is it important for us to share the Body and Blood of Christ?

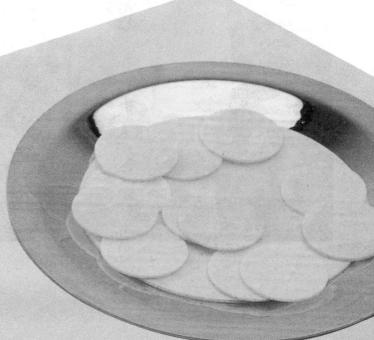

I Have Learned

1. What does the word Eucharist mean?

   _____

2. When did Jesus give us the Eucharist?

   _____

3. What is the celebration of the Eucharist called?

   _____

Prayer

Prayers do not have to be long. Here is a short prayer from the Bible.

Come, Lord Jesus!

I Will Do

When is the next time that you will go to Mass?

Decide now what you will do to prepare better to take part in the Eucharist.

Thank you

Remember

The Eucharist is the sacrament of the Body and Blood of Christ.

When we celebrate the Eucharist at Mass, we are united to Christ and to one another.

The Eucharist is both a meal and a sacrifice.

Review

1. What is the Eucharist?
2. Why do we celebrate the Eucharist?
3. How is the Eucharist a meal and a sacrifice?

4. How can you thank God for the gift of Jesus in the Eucharist?

Family Note

This lesson focuses on the Eucharist as the Body and Blood of Jesus, who gave us the gift of Himself at the Last Supper. You might want to tell or read aloud from the Bible the story of the Lord's Supper (Luke 22:14–20).

9

The Mass

Taking Part

Joan was bored. She was restless, and her mind kept wandering. This often happened when she was at Mass.

Joan wished she were home, listening to music, laughing, playing with friends—anything. But her mom and dad said she had to go to Mass and "take part."

Joan felt her mom's hand touch her shoulder. Joan stopped fidgeting and met her mom's eyes. "Sing," said her mother.

Then she sang "Be...not...afraid...." She nodded for Joan to join in.

Her mom smiled as Joan started to sing. Joan liked to sing. Soon she felt more a part of the celebration. Her mom smiled her encouragement. "That's right," she whispered. "Take part."

What is one way for you to take part at Mass?

VOCABULARY

liturgy
the official public worship of the Church, including the celebration of Mass and the other sacraments

Blessed Sacrament
another name for the Eucharist

Have you ever been bored at Mass?
What do you do about it?

Is there a Mass celebration you especially
remember? Tell about it.

WE WILL LEARN

1 At Mass we listen to God's word.

2 At Mass we offer and receive the gift of Jesus.

3 We bring God's love to others.

1 At Mass we listen to God's word.

The Mass is our celebration of the Eucharist. After God's people have assembled together, the Mass begins. We make the sign of the cross with the priest, who leads our celebration and greets us in Jesus' name. Together, we recall our sins and ask for God's mercy. Then we praise God by saying or singing the Glory to God prayer.

Now we begin the part of the Mass called the *Liturgy of the Word.* During this part of the Mass, we listen to readings from the Bible, the word of God. God speaks to us through these readings. We hear what God has done for us and how God wants us to live.

After the readings, the priest or deacon gives a *homily* and explains their meaning for our lives. Together, we say the Creed, in which we profess our faith in God and in all that the Church teaches. Then we pray together for the needs of the Church, the world, and our local community.

Why is the Liturgy of the Word so important?

For whom or for what would you like to pray the next time you go to Mass?

At Mass we offer and receive the gift of Jesus.

The next part of the Mass is called the *Liturgy of the Eucharist*. We begin the Liturgy of the Eucharist by presenting our gifts of bread and wine to the priest. These gifts are a sign that we give to God all that we are and do. The priest accepts our gifts and prepares the bread and wine for the Liturgy of the Eucharist. Our gifts of bread and wine will become the Body and Blood of Christ.

Then the priest invites us all to join in the Eucharistic Prayer. He says and does what Jesus did at the Last Supper. He says over the bread and wine, "This is my body.... This is my blood...." The bread and wine become the Body and Blood of Christ. This is called the *consecration*. Then in the name of all those present, the priest gives thanks to God by offering up the Body and Blood of Christ. All present sing or say "Amen" as the Eucharistic prayer ends.

Next we pray the Lord's Prayer together as we prepare to receive Christ in Holy Communion. At the proper time, we go to the priest or eucharistic minister and receive Jesus Himself. We receive Communion either in the hand or on the tongue. We do this reverently and with great joy.

What gifts do we offer to God at Mass?

What gift does God give us in return?

Do You Know?

The gifts of bread and wine must be made in a special way because they will become the Body and Blood of Christ. The wine must be made from grapes. The bread is unleavened bread, which does not rise and is made only from wheat and water.

3 We bring God's love to others.

At the end of Mass, the priest blesses us. Then he or the deacon says, "Go in peace to love and serve the Lord."

We try to do this each day by bringing the peace and love of Jesus to everyone we meet. We try to share our time and talents with them. We try to care for the poor, the sick, and the lonely people around us. As members of the Church, we try to bring

God's peace and love to everyone we meet. This is what it means to live the message of the Eucharist we have celebrated and to be followers of Christ.

The next time you go to Mass, how will you take part?

How can you live the Mass in your family? among your friends?

I HAVE LEARNED

Fill in the blanks by choosing the correct answer from among the words listed.

1. The Mass is our celebration of
   _____.

   a. the Church

   b. the Eucharist

   c. Reconciliation

2. God _____ to us in the Liturgy of the Word.

   a. sings

   b. speaks

   c. prays

3. In the Liturgy of the _____, the bread and wine become the Body and Blood of Christ.

   a. Bible

   b. Word

   c. Eucharist

I WILL DO

When you go to Mass this week, listen carefully to the readings during the Liturgy of the Word.

What did you learn in this lesson that will help you to appreciate the Mass more?

PRAYER

The friends of Jesus once came to Him and asked Him to teach them to pray. This is the prayer Jesus taught them.

> Our Father, who art in heaven,
> hallowed be thy name;
> thy kingdom come;
> thy will be done on earth
> as it is in heaven.
> Give us this day our daily bread;
> and forgive us our trespasses
> as we forgive those
> who trespass against us;
> and lead us not into temptation,
> but deliver us from evil. Amen.

Remember

At Mass, we listen to God's word. We offer our gifts of bread and wine and receive the Body and Blood of Christ in Holy Communion. We go from Mass to bring God's love to others.

Review

1. What happens during the Liturgy of the Word?

2. What happens during the Liturgy of the Eucharist?

3. How does God speak to you at Mass? How can you show God your love at Mass?

~~~ Family Note ~~~

This lesson explains the different parts of the Mass. You may want to read this Sunday's gospel with your child and talk about what it means to you. Then encourage your child to be an active participant at Mass. Your example in this will be most important.

Unit III Test

Write the word that best fits each definition.

1. During this sacrament the bishop says, "Be sealed with the Gift of the Holy Spirit."

   _____

2. Through this sacrament, we are made children of God and are freed from sin.

   _____

3. This is our greatest prayer of thanks and praise to God.

   _____

4. This Person of the Blessed Trinity strengthens us with special gifts.

   _____

5. We hear readings from the Bible, the word of God, during this part of the Mass.

   _____

6. This is the belief that there are three Persons in one God.

   _____

7. Each time we celebrate this sacrament, we remember and share in Jesus' sacrifice.

   _____

8. In this, we receive the Body and Blood of Christ.

   _____

9. This is the official public worship of the Church.

   _____

10. During this prayer, the priest says and does what Jesus did at the Last Supper.

   _____

Answer these questions.

11. What is the name of the celebration of the Eucharist?

_____

12. What sacrament strengthens us to be followers of Jesus?

_____

13. What gift does Jesus give us in the Eucharist?

_____

14. When we leave at the end of Mass, what is it we try to bring to others?

_____

15. In Baptism, from what are we freed?

_____

16. When we are confirmed, who comes to us as our Helper and Guide?

_____

17. What is the sacrament that welcomes us into the Church?

_____

18. What sign do we make at the beginning of the Mass?

_____

19. What happens at each celebration of the Eucharist?

_____

_____

20. Why do you think the Mass is the greatest prayer of all?

_____

_____

10

The Ten Commandments

Vocabulary

Ten Commandments
laws given to us by God to help us
live as God's people

Good Rules

The late winter day was already dark when Peter finished basketball practice and started home. Peter was so wrapped up in his thoughts that he did not notice the car until it pulled up beside him.

"Would you like a ride?" the man asked.

Peter looked at him, his heart pumping. All the safety warnings he had heard at home and at school went running through his

mind. He was about to take off down the street when the light went on inside the car. The man repeated. "Peter, can we give you a lift home?"

Peter saw his new friend Mike Lanson waving to him from the passenger seat.

Peter grinned. "Thanks, Mr. Lanson," he said as he climbed into the back seat. "Good for you, Peter," said Mr. Lanson. "You were wise to make sure who we were before getting into the car."

What safety rules do you think Peter had heard at home and at school?

Why do you think people make rules for our safety?

What makes a rule a good rule?

WE WILL LEARN

1 The Ten Commandments tell us how to live as God's people.

2 The first three commandments tell us how to love God.

3 The other seven commandments tell us how to love others and ourselves.

1 The Ten Commandments tell us how to live as God's people.

In the Bible we read that God gave the people of Israel the Ten Commandments, or laws, for their safety and freedom. This is the story of the Ten Commandments.

A long time ago the people of Israel lived as slaves in Egypt. But God had chosen the Israelites to be His own people—the ones who would know and worship the one true God. This was hard for them because they were slaves of the Egyptians who worshiped many false gods. To help the Israelites, God gave them a great leader called Moses.

Moses helped the Israelites escape from Egypt. He led them to safety and freedom in the desert.

In return God asked them to join in a solemn agreement, or *covenant*. God said, "If you will obey Me and keep My covenant, you will be My own people, My chosen people" (from Exodus 19:5). The people promised to obey God and keep the covenant. Then God gave Moses the laws of the covenant called the *Ten Commandments*. The Ten Commandments would help God's people remain faithful to the one true God and be truly safe and free.

The Ten Commandments	What the Commandments Mean for Us
1. I am the Lord your God, who brought you out of slavery. Worship no god except Me.	God must come first in our lives. No one or no thing can be more important to us than God.
2. You shall not misuse the name of the Lord your God.	We must respect God's name, the name of Jesus, and holy places.
3. Remember to keep holy the Sabbath day.	We should rest from work and should worship God together on Sundays and holy days.
4. Honor your father and your mother.	We must love, honor, and obey our parents or guardians.
5. You shall not kill.	We should respect and care for the gift of life.
6. You shall not commit adultery.	We should respect our own bodies and the bodies of others in thought, word, and deed.
7. You shall not steal.	We should not take or destroy what belongs to others.
8. You shall not tell lies against your neighbor.	We should respect the truth.
9. You shall not want to take your neighbor's wife or husband.	We should protect the holiness of marriage and the sacredness of human sexuality.
10. You shall not want to take your neighbor's possessions.	We should respect the rights and property of others.

From Exodus 20:2–17

Name the Ten Commandments. Choose one commandment and explain what it means to you.

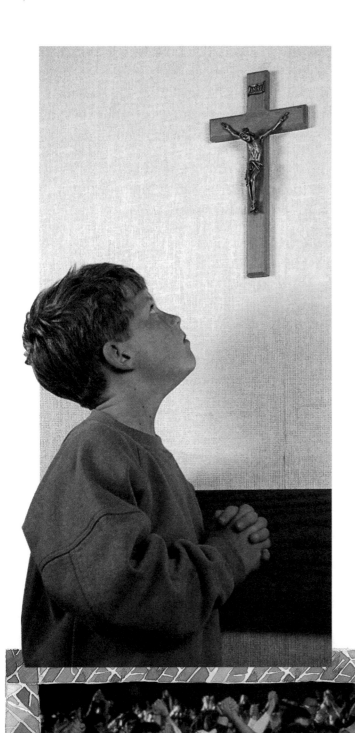

The first three commandments tell us how to love God.

The first commandment tells us that God must come before everyone and everything else in our lives. The second commandment reminds us that God's name is holy and must be used with love and respect.

The third commandment tells us to "keep holy the Sabbath day." The word Sabbath means "rest." For Catholics, Sunday is the Sabbath day. Going to Mass each Sunday is the best way to keep the Sabbath day holy.

How do the first three commandments help you to love God better?

Do You Know?

One day a man asked Jesus which of God's laws was the most important. Jesus answered, "Love the Lord your God with all your heart, with all your soul, with all your mind.... Love your neighbor as you love yourself" (Matthew 22:37–39). We call this the **Law of Love**.

3 The other seven commandments tell us how to love others and ourselves.

The fourth commandment tells us to honor our parents. Because our parents have given us life, we owe them love, respect, and care. We should also show respect for our guardians, our teachers, and older members of the community.

The fifth commandment reminds us that all life is a gift from God. We must not do anything that would harm others, our bodies, or our minds. The sixth and ninth commandments remind us that our sexuality is something sacred. We must respect our bodies and the bodies of others in thought, word, and deed. The seventh and tenth commandments forbid stealing or destroying what belongs to others.

The eighth commandment requires us to tell the truth. It forbids lying and the kind of gossip that hurts others.

Today, the Ten Commandments show us how to remain faithful to God. They help us to live together in peace and love. God has given us these laws for our safety and freedom.

How do these commandments help us to love God and our neighbor better?

I HAVE LEARNED

Choose three commandments. Tell how they help us live as God's people.

PRAYER

At times we pray to thank God for His great gifts to us. Use this prayer to thank God for the laws that help us live in safety and freedom.

> **God, You have given us Your laws**
> **and told us to obey them faithfully.**
> **How I hope that I shall be faithful**
> **in keeping Your laws!**

From Psalm 119:4–5

I WILL DO

The Ten Commandments are not just laws that tell us what we *must not do*. The commandments also tell us what we *must do* to be God's people. Choose one of the commandments. Tell what you will do today or tomorrow to obey that commandment.

Example: Today I will obey the fourth commandment by finding one way to make my family's life happier or easier.

Remember

The Ten Commandments are the laws that God gave us to help us live as God's people.

The commandments help us to love God above all things and our neighbors as ourselves.

Review

1. Name the Ten Commandments.
2. Which commandments require us to love God? Which commandments require us to love our neighbor?

3. How did Jesus answer the question, "What is the most important commandment?"

~ **Family Note** ~

This lesson focuses on the Ten Commandments. Help your child to see that God's laws are meant to free us to live with one another in peace and harmony. Then help your child to learn the Ten Commandments by heart.

11

The Beatitudes

The First Camping Trip

"Tomorrow's the day!" Janet shouted to her friend Rosa as they walked home after school.

"Yep! My sleeping bag is packed, and I'm ready to go," replied Rosa.

Saturday morning they were leaving with the Junior Wilderness Club on their first overnight camping trip. They had been looking forward to it for months.

Later that evening, the phone rang at Janet's. It was Rosa. "I can't go," she whispered.

"What do you mean?" Janet asked.

Rosa told Janet that her mother had gone to the hospital and that she had to stay at home with her grandfather, who could not be left alone. "I hope you'll have a good time. Goodbye, Janet," Rosa said as she hung up the phone.

The next morning Janet was up early. She told her mother what she wanted to do. She put her sleeping bag on her shoulder and left the apartment. She went straight to

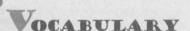

VOCABULARY

Beatitudes
Jesus' guidelines for true happiness

Rosa's house. When Rosa opened the door, Janet said, "I'm not going without you! Let's have our camping trip right here. OK? And we can cook our hot dogs for your grandfather! OK?"

Rosa was so happy she could hardly believe her ears. All weekend the two girls camped at Rosa's house. They helped Rosa's grandfather. And they had fun.

Janet went home feeling great. She said to her mother, "I think happiness is helping someone, isn't it, Mom?" Janet's mother hugged her daughter.

What had Janet expected to do? Do you think she was disappointed?

Have you ever made a decision that:

❖ you thought would make you happy but did not?
❖ you thought would spoil your happiness but instead made it even greater?

WE WILL LEARN

1 Jesus teaches the people about true happiness.

2 The Beatitudes are guidlines for true happines.

3 We try to live with faith, hope and love.

1 Jesus teaches the people about true happiness.

One day Jesus sat on the side of a hill and spoke to the people. He told them not to worry about things— about what they would wear or what they would eat. He said, "Look at the birds of the air. They do not plant seeds, yet your Father in heaven takes care of them. And see how the wild flowers grow. They do not make clothes for themselves, but no king ever had clothes as beautiful as these!"

Then Jesus told the people, "If God cares for these little things, how much more does He care for you! Be concerned above everything else with the kingdom of God and God will take care of all the rest."

From Matthew 6:25–33

The people listened and thought about the lesson of happiness. The way we live will bring us more happiness than what we eat or wear.

2 The Beatitudes are guidelines for true happiness.

Jesus gave the people some guidelines for true happiness. We call these guidelines the *Beatitudes*. Beatitude is a word that means "way to happiness." Each beatitude begins with the word *happy*—a good clue to what the Beatitudes are all about. Look at the chart on page 78. It names the Beatitudes and tells you something about the meaning of each one.

Do You Know?

There are many ways to live as followers of Jesus and be kingdom builders. Missionaries serve God and the Church by bringing the good news of Jesus to the whole world. You can bring the good news to your family, friends, and the people in your parish.

3 We try to live with faith, hope, and love.

The Beatitudes are wonderful guidelines for living as followers of Jesus. They are also surprising because they turn our ideas about happiness upside down. They are not always what we have in mind about being happy! But if we want to be followers of Jesus, we will try to live according to the Beatitudes. To help us do this, God gives us the gifts of faith, hope, and love.

❖ We live as people of *faith* by accepting all that God teaches us. We profess our faith in the Apostles' Creed and the teachings of the Church.

❖ We live as people of *hope* by trusting in Jesus and His promises of the kingdom and eternal life.

❖ We live as people of *love* by loving God above all things and our neighbors as ourselves.

When we live with faith, hope, and love, we gradually come to understand and live the happiness that Jesus was teaching in the Beatitudes.

Name one way you can be a person of faith, of hope, of love.

The Beatitudes	What the Beatitudes Mean for Us
"Happy are those who are poor in spirit; the kingdom of God belongs to them."	People who are poor in spirit depend on God for everything. Nothing becomes more important to them than God.
"Happy are those who mourn; God will comfort them."	People who mourn are saddened by sin, evil, and suffering in the world. They trust that God will comfort them.
"Happy are those who are humble; they will receive what God has promised."	Humble people show gentleness and patience towards others. They will share in God's promises.
"Happy are those who do what God wants; God will satisfy them fully."	People who are fair and just towards others are doing God's loving will.
"Happy are those who are merciful to others; God will have mercy on them."	Merciful people are concerned about others' feelings. They are willing to forgive those who hurt them.
"Happy are the pure in heart; they will see God."	People who keep God first in their lives are pure in heart. They give their worries and concerns to God.
"Happy are those who work for peace; they will be called children of God."	Peacemakers are people who bring peace and reconciliation into the lives of others. They treat others fairly.
"Happy are those who are persecuted because they do what God wants; the kingdom of heaven belongs to them."	People who are willing to be ignored or insulted for doing what they feel God wants will share in God's kingdom.

From Matthew 5:3–10

Choose one beatitude and explain what it means to you.

I HAVE LEARNED

Read the chart on page 78. Choose one of the Beatitudes and tell what it means to you.

I WILL DO

Think of someone you know or have read about who lives according to the Beatitudes. Explain how that person lives the Beatitudes.

What can you do to be more of a "beatitude person" today?

Will you do it?

PRAYER

These words from the prayer of Saint Francis can help us to live as beatitude people.

Lord, make me an instrument of
    Your peace.

Where there is hatred, let me sow love.

Where there is injury, pardon.

Where there is despair, hope.

Where there is sadness, joy.

Remember

Jesus taught us the Beatitudes as guidelines for being truly happy. We try to live the Beatitudes with faith, hope, and love.

Review

1. Name three of the Beatitudes.

2. Choose one beatitude. Tell how you can live this beatitude in your home.

3. Read the last beatitude. Name a time when you will need courage to do what God wants you to do.

Family Note

This lesson emphasizes the Beatitudes and the virtues of faith, hope, and love. Help your child to see that these guidelines enable us to live in peace and harmony with one another.

12

The Sacrament of Reconciliation

VOCABULARY

absolution
the forgiveness of our sins through the words and actions of the priest

sin
freely choosing to do something that we know is wrong, disobeying God's law on purpose

conscience
the ability to know right from wrong

Laurie's Choice

"Some kids say that it's cool to get away with shoplifting at the mall. They say that if you won't even try, you're chicken."

Laurie was talking to her friend Carla on the way home from school. She wondered whether she was missing out on something by never attempting to steal anything in a crowded department store.

"That's not for me," Carla answered. "I know better. Stealing is wrong—whether you get caught or not. It is taking what is not yours."

Laurie still was not sure. She thought about all the kids who said they had taken cassettes or jewelry "just for the fun of it." She wondered whether she should try stealing, too.

If you were Laurie's friend, what would you say to her about shoplifting?

WE WILL LEARN

1 Sin is freely choosing to do what we know is wrong.

2 We examine our conscience before Reconciliation.

3 Reconciliation is a sacrament of God's mercy.

1 Sin is freely choosing to do what we know is wrong.

Everyday we have to make choices or decisions, as Laurie did. Sometimes, we feel like doing something wrong. This is called a *temptation*. A temptation is not a sin. *Sin* is freely choosing to do what we know is wrong. We disobey God's law on purpose.

Some sins are so serious that by doing them we turn away completely from God's love. We call them *mortal sins*. Sin is mortal when:

❖ what we do is very seriously wrong;

❖ we know that it is wrong and that God forbids it;

❖ and we freely choose to do it.

Less serious sins are called *venial sins*. We hurt others and ourselves, but we do not turn away completely from God's love. Venial sins make us less loving members of Jesus' community, the Church.

The Catholic Church teaches us that we can sin in thought, word, or action. We are responsible for our sins and the damage and hurt they cause.

What is the difference between a temptation and a sin?

81

2 We examine our conscience before Reconciliation.

Our conscience helps us to make decisions about what is right and wrong. *Conscience* is the ability to know what is right or wrong, what we should or should not do.

Learning how to make decisions about right and wrong is called *forming our conscience.* We learn to form our conscience by following:

❖ the guidance of the Holy Spirit;

❖ the teachings of the Church;

❖ and the advice of our parents, guardians.

It is important to learn how to *examine our conscience.* This means that we think about our thoughts and actions. We ask ourselves whether we have loved God, others, and ourselves.

3 Reconciliation is a sacrament of God's mercy.

To *reconcile* means to make friends with someone again. When we sin, we need to be reconciled with God. That is why Jesus gave us the sacrament of Reconciliation. In this sacrament we are reconciled with God and the community of the Church. We celebrate God's love and forgiveness and are strengthened to avoid sin in the future.

Before we celebrate the sacrament of Reconciliation, we take time to examine our conscience. Then we confess our sins. This means that we tell the priest the sins we have committed since our last confession. We know that God will forgive our sins if we are sorry.

An Examination of Conscience

In examining our conscience, we ask ourselves questions like these based on the Ten Commandments and the Law of Love.

❖ Have I gone to Mass every week on Saturday evening or Sunday?

❖ Have I used God's name with reverence and respect?

❖ Have I obeyed my parents or guardians?

❖ Have I taken something that belongs to someone else?

❖ Have I done things that are harmful or disrespectful to my body or to the body of someone else?

❖ Have I been truthful and fair?

After the priest listens to our confession, he talks with us about ways we can be better followers of Jesus. He then gives us a *penance* which is a good deed to do or prayers to say. Doing the penance is our way of showing that we are really sorry for the wrong we have done. We pray an Act of Contrition, telling God we are sorry for our sins. The priest then gives *absolution*, or forgiveness. The words and actions of the priest are signs that God has forgiven us.

Two ways of celebrating the sacrament of Reconciliation are the *Individual Rite* and the *Communal Rite.* Both ways of celebrating Reconciliation with the priest are outlined on page 84.

Look at the Individual Rite of Reconciliation. What happens during this celebration?

Look at the Communal Rite. What happens during this celebration?

Whether we celebrate the sacrament of Reconciliation alone or with others, we confess our sins to the priest privately. Then he gives us absolution. This sacrament is a wonderful way to praise and thank God for the gifts of mercy and forgiveness. It is a way to grow in God's grace.

Why do we call the sign of God's love and forgiveness the sacrament of Reconciliation?

Sacrament of Reconciliation

Individual Rite

The priest greets me.

I make the sign of the cross.
The priest asks me to trust in God's mercy.

He or I may read something from the Bible.

I talk with the priest about myself.
I confess my sins: what I did wrong
and why.
The priest talks to me about loving God
and others.
He gives me a penance.

I make an Act of Contrition.
In the name of God and the Church, the
priest gives me absolution. (He may extend
or place his hands on my head.)
This means that God has forgiven my sins.

Together the priest and I give thanks
for God's forgiveness.

Communal Rite

We sing an opening hymn and the priest
greets us.
The priest prays an opening prayer.

We listen to a reading from the Bible and
a homily.

We examine our conscience.
We make an Act of Contrition.

We may say a prayer or sing a song, and
then pray the Our Father.

We confess our sins to a priest. In the name
of God and the Christian community, the
priest gives each of us a penance and
absolution.

We pray as we conclude our celebration.
The priest blesses us, and we go in the
peace and joy of Christ.

I HAVE LEARNED

Number these events in the order in which they happen during the sacrament of Reconciliation.

_____ The priest absolves us from our sins.

_____ We tell our sins to the priest.

_____ We say an Act of Contrition.

_____ The priest gives us a penance.

_____ The priest talks with us about ways that we can better live as followers of Jesus.

I WILL DO

Spend a few minutes of quiet time in a place where you can be alone. Ask God the Holy Spirit for the wisdom to know yourself and to see where you need to improve in your love for God and for others. Just sit quietly, and give God a chance to guide you. Try to do this at least once a week. Act according to what you learn from the Holy Spirit within you.

PRAYER

Trusting in God's mercy, we should tell God that we are sorry for the sins we commit. Here is an Act of Contrition that you can pray.

My God,
I am sorry for my sins
with all my heart.
In choosing to do wrong,
and failing to do good,
I have sinned against you
whom I should love above all things.
I firmly intend, with your help,
to do penance, to sin no more,
and to avoid whatever leads me to sin.
Our Savior Jesus Christ
suffered and died for us.
In his name, my God, have mercy.

Remember

In the sacrament of Reconciliation, we show we are sorry for our sins and receive God's forgiveness through the words and actions of the priest.

Review

1. What is sin?
2. What is mortal sin?
3. What is venial sin?
4. What do we celebrate in the sacrament of Reconciliation?

13

Living as Good Catholics

When Did We See You...?

How do you feel when you watch TV and see pictures of hungry children?

What do you think of when you see someone who is homeless?

Imagine someone who is hungry, thirsty, or homeless. Try to see yourself and your family helping that person. Tell what you would do.

VOCABULARY

Corporal Works of Mercy
ways we care for one another's physical needs

Spiritual Works of Mercy
ways we care for one another's spiritual needs

Sometimes when we see people in need, we feel helpless. "That's terrible," we tell ourselves. But then we ask, "What can I do about it?"

WE WILL LEARN

1 Jesus tells us about the last judgment.

2 Jesus asks us to care for the physical needs of others.

3 Jesus asks us to care for the spiritual needs of others.

Jesus tells us about the last judgment.

Jesus told this story to teach us how we should treat those in need.

At the end of the world, Jesus will come to judge all people. This is called the *last judgment*. To those who have lived justly, He will say, "Come you that are blessed by My Father. I was hungry and you fed Me, thirsty and you gave Me a drink. I was a stranger and you welcomed Me, naked and you gave Me clothes. I was sick and you took care of Me, in prison and you visited Me."

These people will say to Jesus, "Lord, when did we ever do any of these things for You?" Jesus will say, "Whenever you did anything for one of the least important of these brothers or sisters of Mine, you did it for Me."
From Matthew 25:34–40

Jesus used this story to show us how we are to love others.

According to Jesus, when do we ever see Him in need?

Where do you see Jesus today?

Jesus asks us to care for the physical needs of others.

All Christians are called to live lives of justice. Jesus taught us to be fair and to be concerned for the needs of all people. We are to carry out the *Corporal Works of Mercy* as Jesus asks:

* Feed the hungry.
* Give drink to the thirsty.
* Clothe the naked.
* Help those imprisoned.
* Shelter the homeless.
* Care for the sick.
* Bury the dead.

This is how we can make God's kingdom real for all people everywhere.

Which of these Corporal Works of Mercy can people your age do? How?

Do You Know?

As Catholics, we believe that death does not totally and finally separate the living from those who have died. We are all still brothers and sisters in Christ. We can still pray for one another. We call this union of all God's friends—living and dead—the **communion of saints.**

3 Jesus asks us to care for the spiritual needs of others.

To help us care for the spiritual needs of other people, the Catholic Church teaches us the Spiritual Works of Mercy. They are as follows:

✤ Share your knowledge with others.

✤ Give advice to those who need it.

✤ Comfort those who suffer.

✤ Be patient with people.

✤ Forgive those who hurt us.

✤ Give correction to those who need it.

✤ Pray for the living and the dead.

The Corporal and Spiritual Works of Mercy are important practices of our Catholic faith. They remind us that we should live each day as God wants us to live. Following the example of Jesus our Savior and the guidance of the Holy Spirit, we can grow to be strong members of the Church.

Which of these Spiritual Works of Mercy can people your age do? How?

I HAVE LEARNED

Name the Corporal and Spiritual Works of Mercy. In your own words explain what they mean.

I WILL DO

Think of possible slogans to encourage people to do the Works of Mercy.

Choose one slogan and design a bumper sticker for a car or bike. Make copies for your family or friends.

Which slogan will you try to live this week?

PRAYER

Let us pray a prayer of praise to the Blessed Trinity.

**Glory to the Father,
and to the Son,
and to the Holy Spirit.
As it was in the beginning,
is now, and will be for ever.
Amen.**

Remember

Jesus teaches us that whatever we do for others we do for Him.

The Church teaches us how we can serve Jesus in doing the Corporal and Spiritual Works of Mercy.

Review

1. What do we mean by the last judgment?

2. Why should the Corporal and Spiritual Works of Mercy be important for you?

3. Do you find surprising the way Jesus says we will be judged? Why?

Family Note

This lesson focuses on the way we should live as Catholics, practicing the Works of Mercy. Share with your child your own thoughts and feelings about the importance of the Works of Mercy.

14

Mary and the Saints

Faithful Friends

Ben had come over to Lisa's house for some help with his English homework. While Lisa got them some juice out of the refrigerator, Ben looked at the calendar to see when the next English test was scheduled.

"Hey, Lisa, why does your calendar have all these names printed on it?" he asked.

"Those are the names of our saints," Lisa replied. She explained that the Catholic Church honors many of its saints by celebrating their feast days.

> ### VOCABULARY
>
> **rosary**
>   a traditional prayer to Mary
>
> **saint**
>   someone the Church honors as a faithful follower of Jesus

"My mother says it's a nice way to remember our ancestors in God's family," Lisa said. "Isn't that right, Mom?"

"Yes," Lisa's mother answered. "The saints are our friends. They help us and pray for us. That is why parents often name their children after the saints. We named Lisa after Saint Elizabeth."

Do you have a favorite saint?

What do you know about your saint?

WE WILL LEARN

1 Saints help us live as followers of Jesus.

2 Catholics honor Mary as first among the saints.

3 The rosary is one of our best-loved prayers.

1 Saints help us live as followers of Jesus.

Saints are holy people and our brothers and sisters in the Church. During their lives on earth, they tried to follow Jesus in all they said and did. From heaven they continue to watch over and pray for the Church, for all of us. As Catholics, we remember and honor the saints because they show us how we, too, can follow Jesus.

No two saints are exactly alike. Saints have been men, women, or children. Some were married, some not; some were members of religious orders; some were lay people, some ordained. Saints have come from all parts of the world, from every age, and from all walks of life. Martin of Tours, for example, was a soldier; Elizabeth of Hungary was a queen. There were lawyers like Thomas More, and people who gave up everything to follow Christ, as Francis of Assisi and Clare did. There were teachers like Mother Seton, missionaries like Peter Claver, and martyrs like Agnes.

Do you know any stories from the lives of the saints? Share one story.

St. Francis of Assisi

St. Eizabeth of Hungary

2 Catholics honor Mary as first among the saints.

Catholics honor Mary as the greatest of the saints because she is the Mother of God. Here are some things the Church teaches about the Blessed Virgin Mary.

Mary was a young Jewish girl. She faithfully practiced the Jewish religion. God chose Mary to be the mother of the Savior, God's own Son.

The angel Gabriel, God's messenger, came to Mary and said, "You will give birth to a son, and you will name Him Jesus."

Mary was troubled by these words for she was a virgin and not yet married. God promised Mary that the Holy Spirit would come upon her and that her child would be the Son of God.

Mary believed and trusted in God's word. She said, "I am the servant of the Lord. Let what you have said happen to me."

From Luke 1:26–38

Mary became the mother of Jesus, the Son of God. She loved and cared for Jesus all through His life.

The Gospel of John tells us that when Jesus was dying on the cross His mother was there. Many of His followers ran away and hid in fear, but Mary stayed with Jesus until the very end.

Jesus saw His mother and His friend John standing near the cross. He said to Mary, "Here is your son." Then He said to John, "This is your mother" (from John 19:25–27).

The Church tells us that by these words Jesus gave Mary to the whole Church as our mother. That is why we call Mary the Mother of the Church and why she is so important to us.

Why do you think Mary is so important to the Church?

What does Mary mean to you?

DO YOU KNOW?

Many times throughout the year we celebrate our love for Mary. Here are some of them.

Mary, Mother of God—January 1
The Annunciation—March 25
The Visitation—May 31
The Assumption—August 15
The Birth of Mary—September 8
The Immaculate Conception—December 8
Our Lady of Guadalupe—December 12

3 The rosary is one of our best-loved prayers.

One of the ways in which Catholics have shown honor to Mary is through the *rosary*. The rosary is a prayer in which we recall major events in the lives of Jesus and Mary.

The rosary is divided into five groups of ten beads with a single bead set before each group. Each group is called a decade. There is also a crucifix and four other beads at the beginning of the rosary.

We begin the rosary by praying the Apostles' Creed on the cross of the rosary, followed by one Our Father and three Hail Marys. For each decade of the rosary we pray one Our Father, ten Hail Marys, and one Glory to the Father. As we pray each decade, we think about an event, or mystery, from the lives of Jesus and Mary. (The mysteries of the rosary are listed on page 106.)

Explain how to pray one decade of the rosary.

How might the rosary be helpful to you?

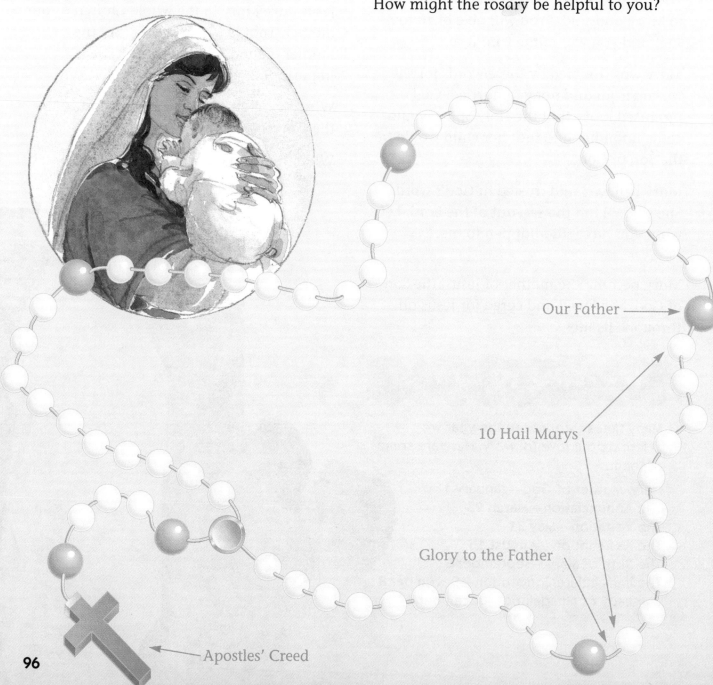

Our Father

10 Hail Marys

Glory to the Father

Apostles' Creed

I HAVE LEARNED

Complete the following statements on Mary and the saints.

❧ Catholics honor Mary because

_____.

❧ When we pray the rosary, we think about

_____.

❧ To me, a saint is someone who

_____.

PRAYER

This is one of the oldest and best loved prayers to Mary.

**Hail Mary, full of grace
the Lord is with you;
blessed are you among women,
and blessed is the fruit
of your womb, Jesus.
Holy Mary, Mother of God,
pray for us sinners now
and at the hour of our death.
Amen.**

I WILL DO

If you do not have a rosary, ask your teacher or parent where you can get one. Spend a few minutes thinking about a favorite event from the life of Jesus and Mary—the birth of Jesus, for example. Then say one decade of the rosary.

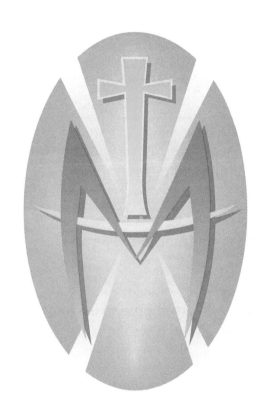

Remember

Catholics honor Mary as first among all the saints.

The saints show us how we can be faithful followers of Jesus.

Review

1. What do we admire in Mary?
2. Why do we honor the saints?
3. What will you do this week to learn more about Mary or one of the other saints?

~~~ Family Note ~~~

This lesson focuses on Catholic devotion to Mary and the saints. Your child has learned that we look to Mary as the mother of Jesus and the model of our spiritual lives. You might give your child a rosary or a picture of a particular saint he or she would like to know more about.

Unit IV Test

Write the word that best completes each definition.

1. The laws given to us by God are the

   _____.

2. Someone the Church honors as a faithful follower of Jesus is a

   _____.

3. Ways we can care for one another's physical needs are the

   _____.

4. A traditional prayer to Mary is the

   _____.

5. To freely choose to do something that we know is wrong is to

   _____.

6. The word *beatitude* means

   _____.

7. The ability to know right from wrong is

   _____.

8. Jesus' guidelines for true happiness are the

   _____.

9. Ways we can care for one another's spiritual needs are the

   _____.

10. A sign of God's forgiveness in Reconciliation is

   _____.

Complete the following quotations with words from the word list. After each quotation, write who said it.

name	Me	kingdom of God	least important
Mine	birth	neighbor	chosen
all	care	covenant	yourself

11. "If you will obey Me and keep My _____ you will be My own people, my _____ people." _____

12. "You will give _____ to a son, and you will _____ Him Jesus."
_____

13. "Love your _____ as you love _____." _____

14. "Be concerned above everything else with the _____ and God will take _____ of _____ the rest." _____

15. "Whenever you did anything for one of the _____ of these brothers or sisters of _____, you did it for _____." _____

Answer the questions on the lines provided.

16. What is the Law of Love?

_____

17. What do the first three commandments tell us?

_____

18. What are the two ways of celebrating the sacrament of Reconciliation?

_____

19. What is the name of the union of all God's friends, living and dead?

_____

20. Think first, then answer this question. For you, what is the most important part of the sacrament of Reconciliation?

_____

_____

Summary Two Test

Circle the correct answer.

1. Each person who wishes to join the Catholic Church must
   a. have Catholic parents.
   b. be a Christian.
   c. be welcomed through Baptism.
   d. have received Holy Communion.

2. After the resurrection of Jesus, His friends often met together to
   a. cry.
   b. pray and celebrate the Eucharist.
   c. be safe.
   d. make a list of new Christians.

3. After we hear the readings from the Bible, the priest or deacon
   a. tells us to leave.
   b. asks us questions.
   c. prays the Our Father.
   d. explains their meaning for our lives.

4. When we examine our conscience before Reconciliation, we
   a. plan how to hurt those who have hurt us.
   b. ask ourselves whether we have loved God, others, and ourselves.
   c. know we are good.
   d. fast for 12 hours.

5. The first three commandments tell us
   a. how bad we are.
   b. how to make friends.
   c. how to love God.
   d. when to sing during Mass.

6. The other seven commandments tell us
   a. to read the Bible daily.
   b. how to love others.
   c. how to pray the rosary.
   d. how to live a long life.

7. We form our conscience by
   a. copying what our parents do.
   b. following our best friend's advice.
   c. learning to make decisions about right and wrong.
   d. reading a good story.

8. The Beatitudes are Jesus' guidelines for
   a. true happiness.
   b. good health.
   c. non-believers.
   d. priests and deacons only.

9. The Corporal Works of Mercy are
   a. what the priest says at the end of Mass.
   b. things our parents make us do at home.
   c. prayers for the dead.
   d. ways we can care for one another's physical needs.

10. The rosary is
    a. a stained-glass window.
    b. a traditional prayer to Mary.
    c. a flower arrangement.
    d. a small chapel.

Answer each question.

11. What happens in the sacrament of Baptism?

_____

12. What is the Mass?

_____

13. What are the Beatitudes?

_____

14. What is the difference between a sin and a temptation?

_____

_____

15. What is a saint?

_____

16. What do the Spiritual Works of Mercy help us to do?

_____

17. Why did God give us the commandments?

_____

18. What does the word *beatitude* mean?

_____

19. Name the steps in the sacrament of Reconciliation.

_____

_____

20. Think first, then answer this question. Jesus said, "Come, follow Me." As a believing Catholic, how are you doing this? (Use another piece of paper to answer this.)

A Doctrinal Review

1 What is the Catholic Church?

The Catholic Church is the community of Christians who become followers of Jesus Christ through Baptism and follow the leadership and authority of the pope and bishops.

2 What is prayer?

Prayer is talking and listening to God.

3 Name the three Persons of the Holy Trinity.

The three Persons of the Holy Trinity are God the Father, God the Son, and God the Holy Spirit.

4 What is original sin?

Original sin is the sin of our first parents in which all of us share.

5 Who is our Savior?

Jesus Christ, the Son of God, who saved us from sin and death is our Savior.

6 What does the word incarnation mean?

Incarnation is the word used to describe the mystery of God becoming one of us in Jesus.

7 What does the word gospel mean?

Gospel is a word that means good news.

8 What happened on Holy Thursday?

On Holy Thursday Jesus shared His last supper with His friends. At that supper Jesus changed bread and wine into His Body and Blood.

9 Why did Jesus suffer and die and rise again to new life?

Jesus suffered and died to save us from sin and death so that we might have eternal life and live forever with God.

10 Who were the apostles?

The apostles were twelve men chosen by Jesus to lead His Church.

11 What happened on the feast of Pentecost?

The Holy Spirit came to the followers of Jesus, filled them with courage and love, and helped them to share Jesus' good news.

12 What are the marks of the Church?

The marks of the Church are one, holy, catholic, and apostolic.

13 Who was the first leader of the Catholic Church?

Saint Peter was the first leader of the Church.

14 ## What is a sacrament?

A sacrament is a powerful sign through which Jesus shares God's life and love with us.

15 ## What is the sacrament of Baptism?

Baptism is the sacrament by which we are freed from sin, become children of God, and are welcomed as members of the Church.

16 ## What is the sacrament of Confirmation?

Confirmation is the sacrament in which the Holy Spirit comes to us in a special way to give us courage to live as Jesus' disciples.

17 ## What is the Holy Eucharist?

The Eucharist is the sacrament of the Body and Blood of Jesus. It is a meal and a sacrifice.

18 ## What is Holy Communion?

Holy Communion is the gift of Jesus Himself under the appearances of bread and wine. When we receive Holy Communion, we receive the Body and Blood of Christ.

19 ## What is the Mass?

The Mass is our celebration of the sacrament of the Eucharist and our greatest prayer of thanks and praise to God.

20 ## What are the Ten Commandments?

The Ten Commandments are laws God gave us to help us live as God's people.

21 ## What are the Beatitudes?

The Beatitudes are Jesus' guidelines for true happiness.

22 ## What is the sacrament of Reconciliation?

The sacrament of Reconciliation is a powerful sign by which we celebrate God's love and forgiveness.

23 ## What is sin?

Sin is freely choosing to do something that we know is wrong. It is disobeying God's law on purpose.

24 ## What are the Corporal Works of Mercy?

The Corporal Works of Mercy are ways we care for one another's physical needs.

25 ## What are the Spiritual Works of Mercy?

The Spiritual Works of Mercy are ways we care for one another's spiritual needs.

26 ## Who is Mary?

Mary is the Blessed Virgin. She is the mother of Jesus Christ, God's Son and our Savior.

The Liturgical Year

The seasons of the liturgical year include Advent, Christmas, Lent, Easter Triduum, Easter, and Ordinary Time. Each season helps us to remember something about the life of Jesus.

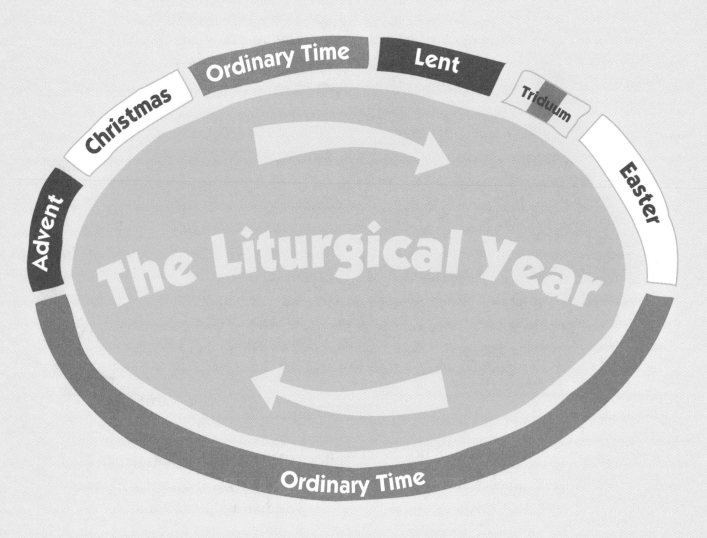

Advent

Advent is a time of preparation for Christmas. We recall the long years when God prepared the world for the birth of Jesus.

The Advent season begins four Sundays before December 25, and ends at the Christmas Vigil Mass. The color of the vestments that the priest wears at this time is violet.

Christmas

Christmas is a time of great joy and love. We celebrate the birth of Jesus, the Son of God.

The Christmas season begins at the Vigil Mass on Christmas Eve and ends on the feast of the Baptism of the Lord. The color of the vestments for this season is white. You may also see gold vestments at this time. These joyous colors symbolize our joyful celebration of the birth of Jesus.

Lent

Lent is a time when we get ready for Easter. During Lent we try to grow closer to Jesus through special prayers and acts of service to our family and other people. It is also a good time to celebrate the sacrament of Reconciliation.

The season of Lent is a period of 40 days that begins on Ash Wednesday, and ends just before the Holy Thursday liturgy. The color of the priest's vestments at this time is violet.

Easter Triduum

The time between the end of Lent and Easter Sunday is called the Easter Triduum. This is a period of three days from Holy Thursday evening until Easter Sunday evening. This is the most important time of the Church year.

Easter

The Easter season begins on Easter Sunday and ends on Pentecost Sunday. The color of the priest's vestments is white or gold. Both of these colors signify the joy of the season of resurrection.

Ordinary Time

All of the other Sundays throughout the year are called Ordinary Time. During Ordinary Time, the readings usually follow a pattern set by a particular gospel. This is done to help us understand more about our faith and the story of salvation. The liturgical color for Ordinary Time is green, the color of hope.

PRAYERS

The Apostles' Creed

I believe in God, the Father Almighty,
creator of heaven and earth.

I believe in Jesus Christ,
his only Son, our Lord.
He was conceived by the power
of the Holy Spirit
and born of the Virgin Mary.
He suffered under Pontius Pilate,
was crucified, died, and was buried.
He descended to the dead.
On the third day he rose again.
He ascended into heaven,
and is seated at the right hand
of the Father.
He will come again to judge
the living and the dead.

I believe in the Holy Spirit,
the holy catholic Church,
the communion of saints,
the forgiveness of sins,
the resurrection of the body,
and the life everlasting. Amen.

Hail, Holy Queen

Hail, Holy Queen, Mother of Mercy,
our life, our sweetness,
and our hope! To you do we cry,
poor banished children of Eve;
to you do we send up our sighs,
mourning and weeping in this
valley of tears. Turn, then,
most gracious advocate,
your eyes of mercy toward us,
and after this our exile,
show us the blessed
fruit of your womb, Jesus.
O clement, O loving,
O sweet Virgin Mary!

Praying the Rosary

The Joyful Mysteries:
- ❖ The annunciation
- ❖ The visitation
- ❖ The birth of Jesus
- ❖ The presentation of Jesus in the Temple
- ❖ The finding of Jesus in the Temple

The Sorrowful Mysteries:
- ❖ The agony in the garden
- ❖ The scourging at the pillar
- ❖ The crowning with thorns
- ❖ The carrying of the cross
- ❖ The crucifixion and death of Jesus

The Glorious Mysteries:
- ❖ The resurrection
- ❖ The ascension
- ❖ The Holy Spirit comes upon the apostles
- ❖ The assumption of Mary into heaven
- ❖ The coronation of Mary in heaven

GLOSSARY

Absolution: The forgiveness of our sins through the words and actions of the priest.

Anointing of the Sick: The sacrament in which God's special blessings are brought to those who are sick, elderly, or dying.

Apostles: Twelve of Jesus' friends chosen by Him to lead His Church.

Ascension: Jesus' return to heaven.

Baptism: The sacrament by which we are freed from sin, become children of God, and are welcomed as members of the Church.

Beatitudes: Jesus' guidelines for true happiness.

Bible: The book in which we read the word of God for our lives.

Bishop: A successor to the apostles in teaching, serving, and leading the Church.

Blessed Sacrament: Another name for the Eucharist.

Blessed Trinity: The three Persons in one God: God the Father, God the Son, and God the Holy Spirit.

Catholic Church: The community of Christians who become followers of Jesus Christ through Baptism and follow the leadership and authority of the pope and bishops.

Communion of saints: The union of all God's friends, living and dead.

Confirmation: The sacrament in which the Holy Spirit comes to us in a special way to give us courage to live as Jesus' disciples.

Conscience: The ability to know right from wrong.

Corporal Works of Mercy: The ways we care for one another's physical needs.

Creator: A name for God who made the universe and everything in it.

Crucifix: A cross with the figure of Jesus on it.

Diocese: A group of parishes that has a bishop as its leader.

Disciple: One who learns from and follows Jesus Christ.

Divine: A word used to describe God alone.

Easter Sunday: The day on which we celebrate the resurrection of Jesus from the dead.

Easter Triduum: The most important time of the Church year. It begins with Evening Mass on Holy Thursday and ends with Evening Prayer on Easter Sunday.

Eternal life: Living forever with God.

Eucharist: The sacrament of the Body and Blood of Christ. It is a meal and a sacrifice.

Examination of conscience: Asking ourselves whether we have loved God, others, and ourselves.

Forming our conscience: Learning how to make decisions about what is right and wrong.

Gifts of the Holy Spirit:

Wisdom—Gives us the power to know what God wants us to do.

Understanding—Helps us to see how Jesus wants us to live in our world.

Right judgment—Helps us to assist others in knowing what is right.

Courage—Helps us to do what God wants, even when we are afraid.

Knowledge—Helps us to know our faith and what is needed to serve God.

Reverence—Helps us to show our love for God in all our thoughts, words, and actions.

Wonder and awe—Helps us to put God first in our lives and to show respect for God's name, the holy name of Jesus, holy places and things.

Good Friday: The day on which we remember that Jesus died for us.

Gospel: The good news of God's love for us.

Gospels: The first four books of the New Testament that describe the life and teachings of Jesus.

Grace: God's life and love in us.

Holy Communion: The gift of Jesus Himself under the appearances of bread and wine.

Holy Orders: The sacrament that confers the ordained ministry of bishops, priests, and deacons.

Holy Spirit: The third Person of the Blessed Trinity who guides and helps the Church.

Holy Thursday: The day on which we remember that Jesus gave us the Eucharist at the Last Supper.

Incarnation: The mystery of God "becoming flesh" or becoming one of us in Jesus.

Justice: Treating all people fairly.

Kingdom of God: The reign, or rule, of God in our hearts.

Last judgment: When Jesus will come to judge all people at the end of time.

Last Supper: The special meal Jesus shared with His friends the night before He died.

Law of Love: The most important of God's laws: to love God with all your heart, soul, and mind and to love your neighbor as yourself.

Liturgy: The official public worship of the Church, including the celebration of Mass and the other sacraments.

Marks of the Church: One, holy, catholic, apostolic; identifying qualities of the Catholic Church.

Mass: Our celebration of the Eucharist and our greatest prayer of thanks and praise to God.

Matrimony: The sacrament that joins a man and a woman together for life.

Mortal sin: A very serious sin that turns us away from God's love.

Original sin: The sin of our first parents in which all of us share.

Parish: A community of Catholics, led by a pastor.

Penance: A way for us to show that we are sorry for our sins.

Pentecost: The day the Holy Spirit came to the followers of Jesus. It is the birthday of the Church.

Pope: The bishop of Rome; the successor to Saint Peter who leads and serves the whole Church.

Reconciliation: The sacrament by which we celebrate God's love and forgiveness.

Resurrection: Jesus' rising from death to new life.

Rosary: A traditional prayer to Mary made up of at least five decades. For each decade we pray one Our Father, ten Hail Marys, and one Glory to the Father.

Sacrament: A powerful sign through which Jesus shares God's life and love with us. There are seven sacraments.

Saint: Someone the Church honors as a faithful follower of Jesus.

Salvation: Freedom from sin and death through the life, death, and resurrection of Jesus Christ.

Savior: Jesus, the Son of God, who saved us from sin and death.

Sign: Something we see, hear, touch, or taste that stands for something else and points to something more important.

Sin: Freely choosing to do something that we know is wrong; disobeying God's law on purpose.

Spiritual Works of Mercy: The ways we care for one another's spiritual needs.

Temptation: A strong feeling to do or want something wrong.

Ten Commandments: The laws given to us by God to help us live as God's people.

Venial sin: A less serious sin that weakens our friendship with God.

Worship: To praise and honor God.

To help us live our Catholic faith each day, we follow the *Laws of the Church.*

1. Celebrate Christ's resurrection every Sunday (or Saturday evening) and on holy days of obligation by taking part in Mass and avoiding unnecessary work.

2. Lead a sacramental life. Receive Holy Communion frequently and the sacrament of Penance, or Reconciliation, regularly. We must receive Holy Communion at least once a year at Lent–Easter. We must confess within a year, if we have committed a serious, or mortal, sin.

3. Study Catholic teaching throughout life, especially in preparing for the sacraments.

4. Observe the marriage laws of the Catholic Church and give religious training to one's children.

5. Strengthen and support the Church: one's own parish, the worldwide Church, and the Holy Father.

6. Do penance, including not eating meat and fasting from food on certain days.

7. Join in the missionary work of the Church.

Certificate of Achievement

_____

(Name)

has successfully completed this study
of the basic beliefs of our Catholic faith.

_____

(Pastor or Teacher)

_____

(Date)